THE
VEGAN
CHEAT SHEET

THE

VEGAN

CHEAT SHEET

**Your Take-Everywhere Guide
to Plant-Based Eating**

AMY CRAMER
and LISA McCOMSEY

A PERIGEE BOOK

A PERIGEE BOOK
Published by the Penguin Group
Penguin Group (USA) Inc.
375 Hudson Street, New York, New York 10014, USA

USA | Canada | UK | Ireland | Australia
New Zealand | India | South Africa | China

Penguin Books Ltd., Registered Offices: 80 Strand, London WC2R 0RL, England
For more information about the Penguin Group, visit penguin.com.

THE VEGAN CHEAT SHEET

ISBN: 978-0-399-16369-2

An application to catalog this book has been submitted
to the Library of Congress.

First edition: July 2013

PRINTED IN THE UNITED STATES OF AMERICA

10 9 8 7 6 5 4 3 2

Text design by Tiffany Estreicher

CONTENTS

FOREWORD

The United States is spiraling downward into debtors' prison faster than any of us can imagine—but nobody seems able to do anything. There is general agreement that the biggest drags on our economy are the entitlements: Social Security, Medicaid, and Medicare. The greatest burden by far is Medicare, and projections indicate that these rising costs will soon be financially unsustainable. Almost half of Medicare expenses derive from a benign food-borne illness—heart disease. In 1998, Chicago economists Kevin M. Murphy and Robert H. Topel estimated that halting heart-disease deaths would save the nation $48 trillion.

For several years, I have been telling audiences that our country is potentially at the cusp of what could become a seismic revolution in health. This revolution will not come about by inventing another pill or building another cardiac cathedral; nor will it arise from a new procedure or operation. Rather, the revolution will come about when we in the medical profession share with the public the lifestyle transition and nutritional literacy that will enable them to avoid developing 75 to 80 percent of the common chronic killing diseases.

Take, for example, coronary artery heart disease, which has been the leading killer of both women and men in the United States for more than fifty years. We know from an epidemiological basis that this disease is virtually nonexistent in cultures whose nutrition—through heritage and tradition—is plant based. Studies of wartime deprivation of animal foods reveal a decline in deaths from heart disease and stroke. In addition, research shows that providing coronary-disease patients with strictly plant-based foods results in the halting, prevention, and even reversal of cardiovascular disease. Positive side effects of a plant-based regime include resolving obesity, hypertension, diabetes, stroke, dementia, and erectile dysfunction.

The challenge is how to educate and persuade the public—which is so steeped in traditional Western disease–producing nutrition—to make the transition to plant based.

Enter Amy Cramer and Lisa McComsey with *The Vegan Cheat Sheet*. These women have artfully and painstakingly crafted a masterpiece, which defines and simplifies the treasured recipes and tastes of plant-based foods. Whether it is the newly initiated or the experienced plant-based devotee, all will find the cuisine creation in this book an epic must-read.

Cramer and McComsey deal with the delicate challenge of eating at friends' houses as well as the daunting task of finding acceptable restaurant nutrition. They have scoured the menus of a multitude of national food chains to identify acceptable choices. Most important, their unique capability of blending produces a host of original, delicious recipes and menus.

The authors have accomplished what many doubters of plant food felt impossible: why not exchange that delicious meal of animal food that sequentially injures you with every mouthful for a delicious plant-based meal that enhances your health with every mouthful?

—Caldwell B. Esselstyn Jr., MD, author of
Prevent and Reverse Heart Disease

INTRODUCTION

Grab Your Fork and Prepare to Eat Your Heart Out, Vegan-Style

Just to set the record straight: We're not masochists. Willpower is not our forte. We hate diets. So now . . . are you ready for your vegan adventure?

For the uninitiated, that means ditching the animal products: no beef, no chicken, no fish, no eggs, no milk, no mayo, no baked Brie, and (saddest of all), no ice cream. Sounds like a fringe diet for weirdos and deprivation junkies, right?

Wrong. The vegan diet is more than lettuce wraps and tofu. As this guide reveals, veganism is not even a diet—it's a way of life that is super easy, fun, and gratifying.

Go ahead: eat your lasagna, your blueberry pancakes, and your Caesar salad. Indulge in family pizza night at Domino's (check our restaurant-ordering secrets for this and other popular chains on page 199). Create mouthwatering meals quickly with our simple, three-step recipes. And, by the way, get your daily dose of nutrients (all that talk about protein-deficient vegans is a bunch of baloney).

What's really cool? You can go vegan in just twenty-one days—because we make the vegan transformation a snap. We—both former omnivores—had to muddle through dozens of books, websites, and magazines to learn the ropes; so now, we've done all the legwork for you.

Here are your menus, your shopping lists, your restaurant guides, your nutrition guide, your travel tips, and more. Everything is packed into one go-everywhere, user-friendly manual that fits in your purse, a pocket, or the glove compartment for quick reference in the restaurant, grocery store, or on the road.

There's no preaching and no tedious data to digest. What resonates is our passion for veganism and our desire to make it accessible to everyone. Want recipes for exotic foods, like pressed cashew cheese and sticky quince cake? You'll have to find those in one of the fancy vegan cookbooks out there, not here.

We keep things simple and tasty: Every recipe can be made in three steps or fewer, generally takes less than twenty minutes hands-on time, and will knock your socks off. Plus, in keeping with Dr. Caldwell Esselstyn's heart-healthy recommendations, we advocate low- or no-fat meals, so all our recipes are free of oils.

Congratulations on your decision to go vegan. Whether you're doing this to get healthy, save the planet, spare a cow's life, or just rebel, you are in for a delicious, nutritious treat!

Caveats

We converted to veganism for health, not ethical, reasons, and we acknowledge that there are varying degrees of the vegan lifestyle. Some vegans, for example, don't consume cane sugar (it's processed with animal-bone char) or honey.

We respect everyone's motivations for going vegan. Because of our chosen vegan path (we *do* eat small amounts of honey and sugar), however, some of our recipes and restaurant-meal recommendations may contain these ingredients. You can easily bypass these selections and find options better suited to your lifestyle.

Also, if you're a heart patient—or you're trying to lose weight—we recommend you steer clear of avocados, chocolate, coconut, nuts, peanuts, and seeds.

1

Our Story

We can hear it now: What? No beef? No chicken? No eggs? No cheese? No milk? No mayo? *No friggin' ice cream?*

What the heck do you weirdos eat, anyway?

Please. We've heard it all. Better yet, we've been there ourselves. Until a few years ago, we were omnivores, too. We relished juicy burgers, sucked down malted milkshakes, and inhaled artisanal cheeses by the truck-load.

And let's not even get into our sweet-tooth problems. Brownies, cookies, cupcakes . . . these were just a few of our favorite things, all oozing with eggs and butter and gooey frostings.

So why on earth did we abandon our favorite foods? "Ah, they must've been plumping up, putting on the pounds," you're thinking. "This was just a quick fix in time for bikini season."

No siree. Actually, we're both exercise fiends who thought we could eat whatever we wanted without expanding our waistlines (ha!).

What happened?

We got scared.

Here's why.

Amy's Story

Popping cholesterol meds for twenty years and coping with their nasty side effects: that was some crazy scary stuff for my husband (the high-cholesterol sufferer) and me. Ken started the medication when he was twenty-eight, and by the time he reached his forties, he was sick of being a cholesterol-drug junkie.

But what were our options? Ken was already a pretty healthy eater—he had sworn off red meat and fatty salad dressing years earlier—and he exercised regularly. Without the drugs, his cholesterol was alarmingly high. With three young kids in tow, we couldn't risk him going off the medication. No, Ken would have to suck it up, side effects or not.

Or so we thought. Until, that is, the night of the party—the night that changed our lives. There, over baked Brie and seven-layer dip, one of the guests told Ken he could ditch the cholesterol drugs by going vegan. Skeptical but intrigued, he threw himself into research mode and read two powerful and compelling books: *Prevent and Reverse Heart Disease*, by Caldwell B. Esselstyn Jr., MD, and *The China Study*, by T. Colin Campbell, PhD.

Once Ken was persuaded to give it a shot, getting me on board was easy. I was a fortysomething fitness and health fanatic who could still (if I do say so myself) rock a bikini. What intrigued me, though, was the culinary challenge. You see, I have always fancied myself a gourmet cook, and I had spent years perfecting French and Italian cuisines. My flourless chocolate torte was the talk of Cleveland. But I had become bored in the kitchen and was itching to learn something new.

So Ken and I decided to try veganism for three months. We also agreed that—in order to keep his cholesterol in check—we would restrict our intake of oils and nuts. While vegan, these products are still fats that should be consumed in moderation.

Day one: instant results! I felt amazing from the get-go. Forgoing my usual breakfast (a heaping bowl of granola-topped yogurt), I prepared a concoction of oats, cereal, fruit, and almond milk. Two hours later, I was still feeling satisfied and energetic; typically by that time, I'd be in "mid-morning drag," feeling sluggish from the dairy.

After two weeks, we knew there was no going back. Ken and I loved the food, the variety, and the results! I was admittedly afraid to step on the scale, since I had reintroduced so many "forbidden" carbs into my diet (all the whole grains and pastas Dr. Atkins deemed verboten). But happily, my bikini fit better than ever, and my husband dropped to his all-time-low high school weight—all this while stuffing our faces.

Within three months, Ken was off the cholesterol meds, and by year's end, I had launched my business as a vegan chef, caterer, and coach (veganeatsusa.com).

What started out as a simple suggestion over a wheel of Brie ended up changing our lives—and my career. I am so excited about how fun, easy, and healthful veganism is—and I can't wait to share it with you!

Lisa's Story

Well, I wasn't scared at first. I was just greedy.

Back in 2009, my family decided we should compete in our own get-fit challenge. The six of us, plus a few of our friends, would set fitness and weight-loss goals and throw $50 each into the till. Whoever achieved his or her goals by the deadline would win the whole pot. I wanted that money *real* bad.

Rewind a few weeks. I had spoken to Amy about her new vegan regimen. Being somewhat of a health and exercise buff, I was intrigued and asked her how to get started. She suggested I read two books, *The China Study* and *Prevent and Reverse Heart Disease*.

That's when I got scared.

The authors are not some hippie-dippy Hollywood flakes but two reformed carnivores—one a former surgeon, the other a doctor of nutritional science. After years of research, both concluded that, in spite of medical advances and the fact that we throw more money at health care than any other society on the planet, Americans are plagued with heart disease, cancer, obesity, diabetes, high cholesterol, and other ills.

Most Americans die from diseases of affluence and overindulgence. If we were to eliminate animal-based products from our diets, the authors say, we would dramatically reduce our risk of succumbing to these health problems. Plant-based foods are the keys to health and longevity.

Oops. At the time, I was eating a bowl of ice cream every night. Pizza was a weekly indulgence. I loved fresh Parmesan cheese so much, I would ask the waiter to grate it over my pasta "until his arm fell off." Coffee with cream and yogurt-infused smoothies were breakfast staples.

Okay, I would try going vegan for a month. You can do anything for a month, right?

Plus, there was that $400 incentive waiting for me if I won the family contest. (I had signed on to lose eight pounds and grunt out twenty boy pushups.)

I was convinced this was a healthy move. But still, there was the question: how on earth was I going to manage? How would I prepare for my month-long challenge?

I found some vegan websites and bought several vegan cookbooks (see Resources, page 237). I stocked my cabinets with exotic herbs and spices: arrowroot, turmeric, cumin, curry, and saffron.

Once addicted to zapping premade frozen meals in the microwave, I began to devote a little more time to preparing fresh dishes. Now exotic delicacies like African stew, Lebanese lentils, and curried butternut squash soup were on the menu. Within a couple of weeks, I felt like a tantalizing new world had opened up, filled with new textures, fragrances, and flavors.

I feel liberated. I love being a vegan! I've never felt better, and I'm always satisfied. My cholesterol dropped forty points, and I ran my twenty-fourth marathon feeling light, energized, and free.

My one-month experiment turned into a way of life that's been easier and more fun than I ever imagined.

So I'm encouraging you to do the same: Take our three-week challenge. Try to go vegan for the next twenty-one days—just twenty-one days—and see how you feel. My bet is you won't go back.

Oh, and by the way, I won the family competition.

Why Anyone
Can Do This

It's So Freakin' Easy, That's Why

We were the unlikeliest of vegans. We loved food and avoided deprivation like the plague. And let's not forget to mention that Lisa is from the Jersey Shore, where pork roll (don't ask) is a revered local dish—best when chased by zeppoles (fried dough balls, rolled in powdered sugar).

We relished omelets (extra cheese, please), pizza (extra cheese, please), and Ben & Jerry's by the pint. When we started reading about the evils of animal products and their role in promoting heart disease, cancer, and other ills that plague the Western world, however, we began to question the whole pork-roll-and-zeppoles thing. Eventually, beef was out and beans were in.

Of course, there were some hardships at first. Lisa pined for cheese. Amy missed her homemade turkey meatballs. The smell of sausage sizzling in the morning still makes us salivate.

But honestly, the cravings dissipate and you find other things that not only satisfy, but also make you feel like a million bucks. When people ask what the biggest difference in how we feel is, we say "clean." Our bodies feel cleansed, healthy, and energized—a far cry from the clogged-up heaviness we felt after pigging out on meat and dairy.

Here's the skinny: we're obsessed with eating. Diets are a drag. So if we can do this, anyone can. Anyone. And that means you!

Why You Should Do This

For Starters, It Could Save Your Life

Let's address the question we get all the time: "Why?" As in, "Why on earth would you kick ice cream, *Brie en croûte*, and Big Macs to the curb?"

Look, we're not scientists. We don't have doctorates in nutrition. But we're voracious readers and researchers, and here's the essence of what we learned when we contemplated going vegan (for all the scientific facts, tests, and data, check the Resources section, page 237):

1. We Americans are fat and getting fatter—which leads to all kinds of health problems. Despite all the "diet" and "health" foods on the market; despite the invasion of gyms on every corner; and despite one of the most respected and sophisticated health-care systems in the world, our health is going down the toilet. Why? Because we eat crap! Even our so-called "diet food" is garbage, filled with sugar, artificial sweeteners, and other junk. Currently, more than one-third of American adults are overweight, and that number is expected to top 40 percent by 2030.

2. Cardiovascular disease is our nation's number-one killer, robbing us of nearly twenty-five hundred men and women a day. That's one person every thirty-three seconds. More people succumb to heart disease than to AIDS and *all* cancers combined. Animal-based products contain all kinds of nasty stuff (fat, cholesterol, and animal protein) that encourages plaque build-up in our arteries (atherosclerosis), which in turn contributes to strokes and heart attacks.

3. Cancer is right behind heart disease as the second-leading cause of death—and it's expected to usurp the number-one spot in a few years. One in three people will contract cancer in his or her lifetime, and one in four will die from it. With odds like these, many of us just throw up our hands, cross our fingers, and hope for the best, thinking we have no control over our cancer destinies. Ah, but we do! Open your fridge. Peek inside your cabinets. Examine your dinner plate. What you see may be hurting you, big time. Many forms of cancer thrive on our staples—dairy, meat, and eggs—as well as our vices—processed sugar, tobacco, and alcohol. Plant-based foods, with their fiber, phytochemicals, and antioxidants, can help the body ward off cancer cells.

4. Other diseases, like diabetes and Alzheimer's, can be helped or prevented by embracing a plant-based diet. In studies, diabetics who adopted a vegan diet experienced weight loss, improved blood-sugar levels, lower cholesterol, and better kidney function. Alzheimer's research suggests that those who consume fat- and cholesterol-laden meats and dairy products are likelier to develop Alzheimer's than their plant-eating counterparts.

5. The animals will thank you. Some former carnivores we meet say they don't care as much about their cholesterol as they do about the brutal exploitation of animals that are slaughtered (to the tune of 27 million a year in the United States), maimed, and otherwise mistreated for our consumption. For them, that is reason enough to go vegan. If that's your motivation, we applaud you.

4

Vegan Myth Versus Truth

There are a lot of vicious rumors circulating about the vegan diet. Here, we dispel them one by one.

MYTH: A vegan diet is nutrient deficient.

TRUTH: Fruits, vegetables, beans, and grains—the staples of a vegan diet—are crammed full of vitamins, minerals, and all kinds of good, healthy stuff. So vegans who eat a well-balanced and varied diet can get all the nutrients they need, including (much to people's surprise) iron and protein. The American Dietetic Association's position is that "appropriately planned vegan diets are healthful, nutritionally adequate, and may provide health benefits in the prevention and treatment of certain diseases." One vitamin we like to pop every day is B_{12}, since that's a little tougher (but not impossible) to derive from plant-based foods; nutritional

The Dirt on Protein

Hands down, the question we're asked most frequently is, "How do you people get your protein?" Well, it's super easy. You don't need a slab of beef or a bucket of fried chicken to reap your daily allotment. Nope, plant protein is abundant and—unlike meat—has the added benefit of being fiber-rich and cholesterol-free. Toss some grains, legumes, nuts (in moderation), seeds, veggie burgers, tofu, and protein-packed vegetables down the hatch, and your body will be well supplied with protein. Take that, carnivores! For a list of sources of plant-based protein, see page 45.

yeast and many nondairy beverages, cereals, and meat substitutes are fortified with B_{12}. (For more on B_{12}, see page 30.)

MYTH: With such limited food choices, I'll die of boredom.

TRUTH: If you think the vegan lifestyle is boring and restrictive, you're in for a delicious surprise. Once you break up with animal products, you'll kiss food hangovers good-bye and discover a whole new world of foods and flavors. Mealtime becomes exciting and adventuresome. Plus, with the increasing popularity of veganism, you'll find more and more options on your grocery store shelves. Afraid you'll never be able to eat lasagna again? Check out Amy's recipe on page 108. You won't miss the fatty, beefy version one bit. Besides, what's so darn exciting about eating meat and potatoes every day anyway? Talk about boring!

MYTH: I'm into health, but deprivation's not my bag. I can't do a restrictive diet.

TRUTH: What we love most about the vegan lifestyle (no, it's not a diet) is that we eat. And eat. And eat. We pretty much eat whatever we want, whenever we want it. People are aghast at the amount of chow we can put away. When you consume healthy vegan foods, you don't have to measure portions or count calories. Now, that's liberating! A word of caution: it *is* possible to be a

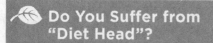

Do You Suffer from "Diet Head"?

You know how even the word *diet* makes you want to cheat? Even though we were pretty healthy eaters prior to going vegan, there were times we wanted to lose weight and would go on this or that fad diet. But any type of food denial made us instantly crave sundaes, birthday cake, and french fries, and the diet was doomed to fail. So when we first became vegans, we feared living in a perpetual state of "diet head." But a funny thing happened. Our new vegan brains rarely even think of eating the verboten foods—not because we can't, but because we choose not to. There are so many delicious foods to discover; we're always so satisfied and we feel so darn good that we don't want to go back to the old way of eating.

vegan chubbette—hitting the potato chip bag, overdosing on vegan cupcakes, or living on chocolate and peanut butter can pack on the pounds. Eat those in moderation.

MYTH: Going vegan is expensive.

TRUTH: You'll actually save money. During the learning process, you may find yourself making a small investment as you buy and try new things (we actually saw our grocery bills nosedive, but that varies depending on what ingredients and equipment you already have sitting in your kitchen). And once you've really settled in to the lifestyle, you'll discover that eating a plant-based diet is cheaper than forking over money for cheese, beef, and other meaty products. Also, many vegan staples—like grains, beans, and pastas—are easy on the wallet and have long shelf lives, so there's little risk of food spoilage and waste. And how about this bonus: given your healthy new eating habits, you're likely to save a bundle on medical bills. Take that to the bank!

MYTH: Going vegan is a pain in the butt.

TRUTH: Once you figure out how to substitute plant-based foods for animal products, the inconvenience will go the way of your liverwurst-and-onion sandwich. Really, now: is it that hard to order marinara sauce instead of Alfredo sauce? Or swap a bean burger for a bacon cheeseburger? Or replace half-and-half with coconut creamer in your morning Joe? Sure, there's a break-in period, but once you get the hang of it, you'll be rocking veganism like it's nothing. And if you prefer to adopt the vegan diet gradually as opposed to swearing off animal products cold turkey, that's cool. Start by eliminating a few things and keep adding to the list until you're a full-fledged plant eater. Or, pick certain days of the week to go vegan (thanks to Oprah, "Meatless Mondays" have taken off), until you've nailed all seven days.

MYTH: I live in the burbs, where those fancy organic stores don't dare venture. I'll never be able to buy the foods I need.

TRUTH: Lisa here. I sympathize—I live in one of those places, too. (I dream of the day a Whole Foods or Trader Joe's will materialize in my Jersey town.) But you know what? Much to my amazement, I've been able to find the most oddball vegan-friendly foods at my local grocery store. More and more mainstream chains are starting to carry products that cater to people's dietary needs, like vegan, organic, and gluten-free. And, of course, all grocery stores stock fruits, vegetables, beans, grains, and tons of other vegan-friendly stuff. I fill in the blanks at my neighborhood health-food store. And if all else fails? I rely on the purveyor of absolutely everything, the Internet, to order whatever I need—from teff grain to chia seeds to nutritional yeast. Some great online options:

- Amazon (amazon.com) stocks most things
- Bob's Red Mill (bobsredmill.com) offers flours, cereals, grains, beans, and seeds
- Pleasant Hill Grain (pleasanthillgrain.com) supplies grains, beans, and legumes

MYTH: I'm so lame. I tried eating vegan but caved to a buttercream-frosted cupcake last night. That's a smudge on my vegan record. I can't go back.

TRUTH: So what you're saying is . . . you're human? Welcome to our world! While we're darn good vegans, we're not perfect, either. And because we choose this lifestyle for health reasons, we may allow ourselves the occasional small breach. (Sorry, but if there's a buttercream-frosted cupcake in the vicinity, Lisa must have a bite. And just try holding Amy back from a nibble of chocolate *anything*.) If you choose veganism for ethical reasons—or if you're a heart patient—such allowances may not be acceptable to you. But anyone can fall off the wagon, either knowingly or unknowingly. Just get over it and hop back in the saddle.

MYTH: Vegans are weird.

TRUTH: There are weird carnivores. And there are weird vegans, sure. But the stereotype that vegans are militant, Birkenstock-clad hippies who parade around in bamboo socks and sport "Meat is Murder" bumper stickers is not necessarily true. Take us, for example. We're not that weird. Like many vegans, we buy normal clothes at normal department stores, eat normal (vegan) food at normal restaurants, and befriend normal carnivores. We pretty much blend in with everyone else except for the fact that, well, we don't eat animal products. Here are some vegans you may have heard of (you decide whether they're weird or not):

Alanis Morissette	Bryan Adams
Alec Baldwin	Carl Lewis
Alicia Silverstone	Carrie Underwood
Anthony Kiedis	Chelsea Clinton
Bill Clinton	Ellen DeGeneres
Brad Pitt	Jason Mraz

Lea Michele	Shania Twain
Mike Tyson	Ted Danson
Moby	Venus Williams
Natalie Portman	Weird Al Yankovic
Portia de Rossi	Woody Harrelson

Okay, some of them are definitely weird. But fame can do that to a person.

MYTH: I need to follow a gluten-free diet. I can't juggle two hard-core eating regimens at once.

TRUTH: First of all, both eating styles can be delightful, easy, and fun. Secondly, it's super simple to be a gluten-free vegan. In fact, most of our recipes are gluten-free. Also, be sure to check out our Great Grains chapter (page 46) for a host of delicious gluten-free choices.

MYTH: Vegans are skinny, sickly-looking weaklings.

TRUTH: Hello, have you seen us? Well, probably not, but just so you know: we've got curves! We run marathons! We bike! We hike! We've aced two-minute planks and downward-facing dogs! We lift weights! And by the way, our goal is not to be skinny. We strive to be fit and healthy. We like having hips and butts. Enough said?

5

A Few Words
of Advice

DON'T BLOAT AWAY

Your fibrous new diet may stir up gassiness and bloating, so pick up a natural supplement—such as Beano—to quell your potential toot boost. Or simply arrange to dodge your friends until things settle down. (And enjoy your newfound regularity!)

POP B_{12}

A well-balanced vegan diet is naturally rich in every nutrient except B_{12}, which comes primarily from animal products. We recommend taking a B_{12} supplement (check with your physician first). It can also be found in some fortified cereals, soy products, and nutritional yeast.

The Scoop on B$_{12}$

A lot of fuss is made about B$_{12}$ and veganism, since animal products are its primary source. While vitamin B$_{12}$ deficiency is not common among vegans, extremely low intake can cause anemia and damage to the nervous system. The body needs limited doses (these vary depending on your age and health)—which are easily obtained through fortified foods, supplements, and nutritional yeast.

CHANGE OUT THE OIL

In keeping with Dr. Caldwell Esselstyn's recommendation to restrict fats and oils, we don't incorporate any oils into our recipes. According to Dr. Esselstyn, there's no such thing as "heart-healthy oil." Even the highly revered olive oil—a staple in the Mediterranean diet—contains up to 17 percent saturated, artery-clogging fat, which can do as much damage as the saturated fat in roast beef. We do, however, occasionally use seeds, nuts, and avocados, which he advises his heart patients to avoid. So if you are battling a cardiovascular condition, please eliminate those ingredients or bypass those dishes altogether.

CLEAR OUT THE JUNK

Reformed ice-cream-aholics, we sure love a treat now and then. But we don't sit around stuffing our faces with potato chips, fried onion rings, and gummy worms, then wash them all down with a gallon of soda. While it's possible to be a plump, junk food–addicted vegan, we advocate eating the healthy stuff. If your sweet tooth is aching for a fix or if you're hankering for some fries with that veggie burger, go for it now and then. Just try to do it sparingly. Or indulge in one of the healthier treats in our recipe section, beginning on page 168.

PROMOTE DIVERSITY

To get the biggest bang for your nutrient buck, be sure to eat a wide variety of foods. A diverse and colorful diet will help you meet your vitamin, mineral, and protein needs. Put these on the menu:

- Fruits and vegetables of every color—green, orange, pink, purple, red, white, and yellow
- Legumes—including beans, lentils, and peas
- Grains—such as barley, brown rice, oats, quinoa, wheat berries, and wild rice (check out our Great Grains chapter on page 46 for some toothsome choices, along with preparation instructions for each)
- Whole-grain breads, cereals, and pastas (scrutinize labels for fats, dairy, and eggs); make sure these products are 100 percent whole grain
- Nuts (in moderation; avoid if you're a heart patient)—almonds, Brazil nuts, macadamia nuts, pecans, and walnuts
- Seeds (in moderation; avoid if you're a heart patient)—chia, flax, pumpkin, sesame, and sunflower

STUDY YOUR LABELS

While the vegan diet is rich in fresh fruits and vegetables, there are still times you will need to buy canned, packaged, or prepared foods. When you do, be sure to read the ingredient labels to check for unexpected animal additives, like dairy, chicken or beef broth/stocks, eggs, and so forth. Several brands of veggie burgers, for example, contain eggs, while some soy cheeses are made with dairy.

Beware animal ingredients in disguise, like:

- **Albumen**—Derived from milk or egg whites, albumen is used as a food binder in soups and baked goods.
- **Casein**—The main protein in cow's milk, it comes in several forms, which may be listed as ammonium caseinate, calcium caseinate, potassium caseinate, or sodium caseinate. Casein is used for making cheese and to enhance the texture of foods, including cereals, breads, and chocolates.
- **Gelatin**—Used to make treats like Jell-O, gummy bears, and marshmallows, gelatin is made by boiling the skin, tendons, ligaments, and/or bones of cows and pigs (kosher gelatin is made from fish).
- **Lard**—This pig fat is occasionally used in cooking and baking.
- **Lecithin**—Some lecithin is derived from animal fat and eggs (soy lecithin is made from soybeans); it's used as an emulsifier and is often found in salad dressings to prevent separation of oil and vinegar.

- **Rennet**—Extracted from the stomach of calves, rennet is used as a coagulant in the cheese-making process.
- **Whey**—The remaining liquid after milk curds are separated out, whey is used to make cheese and is often found in protein energy bars.

6

Your Daily Dose

Forget all that hogwash about vegans being nutrient deprived. Everything our systems need to function is conveniently found in plant-based foods. Here's a checklist of the vitamins and minerals you need to maintain a shipshape body—and where in the plant world you can find them.

CAVEAT: If you're a heart patient—or you're trying to lose weight—avoid avocados, chocolate, coconut, nuts, peanuts, and seeds. Everyone else should consume these in moderation.

Vitamins

Vital to our growth, vitality, and overall health, vitamins are essential to the proper functioning of the human body. Each of the thirteen vitamins plays a specific role and can be obtained from various food sources.

VITAMIN A

Vitamin A promotes good eyesight, thwarts night blindness, helps fight infection, and aids in bone and tissue development and repair.

Select Sources of Vitamin A

- Dark leafy greens—collard greens, dandelion greens, kale, mustard greens, red-leaf lettuce, salad greens, spinach, and turnip greens
- Dried fruits—apricots
- Fruits—cantaloupe and mango
- Herbs (dried)—basil, dill, marjoram, oregano, and parsley

 Kale: The Queen of Greens

While no beauty, this super vegetable has far more to offer than good looks—and is definitely prettier than, say, cauliflower. What we love about kale is what's inside: a nutritional power-house that's low in calories (just thirty-six per cup), high in fiber, and devoid of fat. It's brimming with vitamins A, C, and K, and boasts more iron per calorie than beef and more calcium per calorie than milk. If that weren't enough, kale provides about 10 percent of the RDA for omega-3 fatty ac-ids, making it a killer antioxidant, too.

- Juice—tomato
- Nuts—pistachios
- Vegetables—broccoli, butternut squash, carrots, pumpkin, red peppers, summer squash, and sweet potatoes
- Spices—cayenne, chili powder, and paprika

B VITAMINS

Vitamin B$_1$ (Thiamine)

Essential for proper functioning of the heart, muscles, and nervous system, vitamin B$_1$ helps convert carbohydrates into energy and contributes to healthy hair, skin, eyes, and liver.

Select Sources of Vitamin B$_1$

- Brewer's yeast
- Dark leafy greens—kale, romaine lettuce, and spinach
- Fortified whole-grain breads, cereals, and pastas
- Fruits—cantaloupe, grapes, oranges, pineapple, and watermelon
- Herbs (dried)—coriander, mustard seeds, paprika, rosemary, sage, and thyme
- Juice—orange
- Legumes—black beans, green peas, kidney beans, lentils, lima beans, navy beans, peanuts, pinto beans, soybeans, and split peas
- Nutritional yeast
- Nuts—Brazil nuts, macadamia nuts, pecans, pine nuts, and pistachios
- Seeds—poppy, sesame, and sunflower

- Vegetables—asparagus, bell peppers, broccoli, carrots, cauliflower, celery, corn, green beans, and mushrooms
- Whole grains—oat bran, wheat bran, and wheat germ

Vitamin B$_2$ (Riboflavin)

Playing a key role in helping the body metabolize fats and proteins, vitamin B$_2$ is also essential for healthy skin, hair, eyes, and liver, and helps the nervous system function optimally.

Select Sources of Vitamin B$_2$

- Dark leafy greens—collard greens, dandelion greens, kale, romaine lettuce, spinach, Swiss chard, and watercress
- Fruits—avocado, currants, plums, raspberries, and strawberries
- Herbs (dried) and spices—ancho chilies, chili powder, coriander, paprika, parsley, sage, and spearmint
- Legumes—lima beans, navy beans, peas, and soybeans
- Molasses
- Nuts—almonds
- Seeds—sesame
- Vegetables—asparagus, artichokes, broccoli, Brussels sprouts, mushrooms (especially cremini), pumpkin, sundried tomatoes, and sweet potatoes
- Whole grains—quinoa, wheat bran, and wild rice
- Whole-grain and enriched breads, cereals, and flours

VITAMIN B$_3$ (NIACIN)

Vitamin B$_3$ helps with the functioning of the digestive system, skin, and nerves and contributes to overall health and growth.

Select Sources of Vitamin B$_3$
- Brewer's yeast
- Dark leafy greens—collards, kale, spinach, and watercress
- Fortified whole-grain breads, cereals, and pastas
- Dried fruits—apples, apricots, dates, and raisins
- Fruits—apples, apricots, avocado, bananas, blackberries, blueberries, cantaloupe, figs, honeydew, mangos, peaches, pears, pineapple, plums, and watermelon
- Legumes—black beans, chickpeas, fava beans, Great Northern beans, kidney beans, lima beans, navy beans, and peanuts
- Nuts—almonds
- Seeds—sunflower
- Spices—paprika
- Vegetables—asparagus, beets, broccoli, cabbage, carrots, celery, corn, mushrooms, sweet potatoes, tomatoes, and turnips
- Whole grains—rice bran, spelt, wheat bran, and wheat germ

VITAMIN B$_5$ (PANTOTHENIC ACID)

Like other B vitamins, B$_5$ helps the body synthesize and metabolize fats, proteins, and carbohydrates. It also aids with red blood cell production; keeps the gastrointestinal system running smoothly; and promotes healthy skin, muscles, and nerves.

Select Sources of Vitamin B$_5$

- Brewer's yeast
- Dark leafy greens—collard greens and kale
- Dried fruits—prunes
- Fruits—avocado, bananas, blackberries, cherries, oranges, peaches, pineapple, and strawberries
- Legumes—peanuts and peanut butter, peas, and soybeans
- Nuts—almonds, chestnuts, and hazelnuts
- Seeds—sunflower
- Vegetables—broccoli, carrots, cauliflower, corn, cucumber, mushrooms, parsnips, squash, sun-dried tomatoes, sweet potatoes, and zucchini
- Whole-grain breads, cereals, and pastas
- Whole grains—brown rice, rice bran, wheat bran, and wheat germ

VITAMIN B$_6$

The body uses vitamin B$_6$ to process proteins, fats, and carbohydrates, and to help promote a healthy immune system and new cell growth.

Select Sources of Vitamin B$_6$

- Brewer's yeast
- Dark leafy greens—collard greens, dandelion greens, kale, and spinach
- Dried fruits—prunes
- Fruits—bananas and cantaloupe
- Legumes—chickpeas, lima beans, peanuts, peas, and soybeans

- Nuts—cashews, hazelnuts, and walnuts
- Seeds—sunflower
- Vegetables—asparagus, broccoli, Brussels sprouts, cabbage, carrots, cauliflower, green beans, mushrooms (cremini), peppers (red and green), and potatoes (baked with skin)
- Whole grains—wheat germ
- Whole-grain cereals

VITAMIN B$_9$ (FOLATE OR FOLIC ACID)

Along with vitamins B$_{12}$ and C, folic acid aids with digestion, red blood cell production, and DNA synthesis. It also contributes to healthy tissue growth and cell function and helps lower the risk of stroke, cancers, heart disease, and possibly Alzheimer's.

Select Sources of Folate
- Dark leafy greens—collard greens, dandelion greens, romaine lettuce, spinach, and turnip greens
- Fortified whole-grain breads, cereals, and pastas
- Fruits—avocado, bananas, blackberries, cantaloupe, papaya, and strawberries
- Juices—orange and tomato
- Legumes—black-eyed peas, chickpeas, kidney beans, lentils, lima beans, navy beans, peanuts, pigeon peas, pink beans, pinto beans, split peas, and white beans
- Nondairy milk—soy and folate-fortified nondairy milks
- Seeds—sunflower
- Vegetables (cooking can reduce folate content; when possible, try to eat these raw)—artichokes, asparagus, beets, broccoli, Brussels sprouts, cauliflower,

corn, endive, fennel, okra, onions, parsnips, peas, peppers, potatoes, radicchio, and radishes
- Whole grains—wheat bran

VITAMIN B$_{12}$

Essential for healthy skin, hair, and nails, vitamin B$_{12}$ also helps protect against anemia, fatigue, weakness, constipation, loss of appetite, depression, poor memory, asthma, vision problems, and low sperm count.

Select Sources of Vitamin B$_{12}$
- Fortified whole-grain cereals
- Fortified nondairy milks
- Nutritional yeast

BIOTIN

This B vitamin is essential for proper growth and metabolism of food.

Select Sources of Biotin
- Brewer's yeast
- Fruits—avocado, bananas, papaya, strawberries, and raspberries
- Dark leafy greens—romaine lettuce and Swiss chard
- Legumes—peanuts and soybeans
- Nuts—almonds, cashews, hazelnuts, and walnuts
- Vegetables—cabbage, carrots, cauliflower, cucumber, mushrooms, sweet potatoes, and tomatoes
- Whole grains—oats, rice, and wheat
- Whole-grain cereal

VITAMIN C

Best known for its ability to fight colds and strengthen the immune system, vitamin C is a powerful antioxidant that also promotes cellular health and may help guard against cardiovascular disease, prenatal health problems, cataracts, and skin wrinkling.

Select Sources of Vitamin C

- Citrus fruits—grapefruit, lemons, limes, oranges and tangerines
- Dark leafy greens—kale, mustard greens, turnip greens, spinach, Swiss chard, and watercress
- Fruits—blackcurrants, blueberries, cantaloupe, cherries, guava, kiwifruit, mango, papaya, pineapple, raspberries, strawberries, and watermelon
- Herbs (fresh)—basil, chives, cilantro, parsley, and thyme
- Juices—grapefruit, guava, orange, tangerine, and tomato
- Vegetables—broccoli, cauliflower, potatoes, sweet peppers, and tomatoes

VITAMIN D

Naturally derived from sunlight, vitamin D helps the body absorb calcium and phosphorus, which are needed for strong bones.

Select Sources of Vitamin D

- Fortified nondairy milks
- Fortified whole-grain breakfast cereals
- Juice—orange (fortified)

- Vegetables—mushrooms (the only vegetable source of this vitamin!)
- The sun (limited daily exposure)

VITAMIN E

Packed with antioxidant benefits, vitamin E helps prevent cancer, heart disease, strokes, cataracts, and possibly some signs of aging.

Select Sources of Vitamin E
- Dark leafy greens—beet greens, dandelion greens, spinach, and turnip greens
- Fortified whole-grain breakfast cereals
- Fruits—avocado, kiwifruit, mango, and papaya
- Legumes—peanuts and peanut butter
- Nuts—almonds, hazelnuts, and pine nuts
- Seeds—sunflower
- Vegetables—asparagus, pumpkin (canned), red peppers, and tomatoes
- Whole grains—wheat germ

VITAMIN K

The often-overlooked vitamin, K is essential to blood clotting, bone health, and brain function and has anti-inflammatory benefits.

Select Sources of Vitamin K
- Dark leafy greens—beet greens, collard greens, dandelion greens, kale, mustard greens, romaine lettuce, spinach, Swiss chard, and turnip greens
- Dried fruits—prunes
- Fruits—avocado, blackberries, blueberries, figs, and grapes

- Vegetables—broccoli, Brussels sprouts, endive, and scallions

Minerals

Essential to a healthy diet, minerals are naturally occurring nutrients found in inanimate things like rocks, metals, and soil. Plants derive their minerals from the ground, which in turn are passed on to us when we ingest them.

CALCIUM

Calcium is essential for strong bones and teeth, contributes to proper blood clotting, and aids in muscle and nerve health.

Select Sources of Calcium
- Blackstrap molasses
- Dark leafy greens—bok choy, broccoli, collard greens, dandelion greens, kale, mustard greens, rhubarb, romaine lettuce, spinach, and turnip greens
- Dried fruits—apricots, dates, and figs
- Fortified nondairy milks
- Fruits—blackberries, blackcurrants, and oranges
- Juice—orange (fortified)
- Legumes—black beans, chickpeas, lentils, lima beans, navy beans, pinto beans, soybeans, soy nuts, split peas, and white beans
- Nut and seed butters—almond, sesame, and sunflower
- Nuts—almonds, hazelnuts, and walnuts
- Seeds—sesame and sunflower
- Some tofu (check nutrition label)

- Vegetables—artichokes and broccoli
- Whole grains—amaranth, brown rice, cornmeal, oats, and quinoa

CHLORIDE

An essential component of digestive juices, chloride also helps regulate the balance of fluid in the blood vessels and cells.

Select Sources of Chloride
- Olives
- Table salt (use in moderation)
- Vegetables—celery, lettuce, seaweed, and tomatoes

CHROMIUM

This essential trace element, though needed in small amounts, plays a major role in helping to stabilize blood-sugar levels and metabolize fat, carbohydrates, and protein.

Select Sources of Chromium
- Brewer's yeast
- Dark leafy greens—romaine lettuce and spinach (cooked)
- Dried fruits—prunes
- Fruits—apples and bananas
- Herbs and spices—black pepper and thyme
- Juices—apple, grape, and orange
- Legumes—peanuts
- Molasses
- Vegetables—asparagus, beets, broccoli, corn, garlic, green beans, green peppers, mushrooms, raw onion, sweet potatoes, and tomatoes

- Whole grains—wheat germ
- Whole-grain cereals and breads

COPPER

An essential trace mineral, copper is critical in the formation of red blood cells. Found in all body tissues, it helps keep blood vessels, nerves, bones, connective tissue, and the immune system healthy.

Select Sources of Copper
- Blackstrap molasses
- Cocoa
- Dark leafy greens—beet greens, kale, mustard greens, spinach, Swiss chard, turnip greens, and watercress
- Dried fruits—pears and prunes
- Fruits—avocado and cherries
- Herbs—basil
- Legumes—chickpeas, navy beans, and soybeans
- Nuts—cashews
- Seeds and seed butters—pumpkin, sesame, and sunflower
- Spices—black pepper
- Tempeh
- Tofu
- Vegetables—asparagus, eggplant, mushrooms (cremini), Napa cabbage (cooked), potatoes, radishes, summer squash, and tomatoes (canned and fresh)
- Whole grains—barley

FLUORIDE

Small amounts of fluoride can help prevent tooth decay, cavities, and osteoporosis. This mineral also promotes strong teeth and bones.

Select Sources of Fluoride
- Fluoridated tap water and foods prepared with fluoridated tap water
- Fluoride toothpastes and rinses
- Tea

IODINE

An important mineral needed in low doses, iodine helps the body metabolize nutrients and is essential for healthy development and growth.

Select Sources of Iodine
- Iodized salt (use in moderation)
- Plants grown in iodine-rich soil
- Seaweed

IRON

An essential mineral, iron helps transport oxygen throughout the body and works to maintain healthy cells, skin, hair, and nails. Note: There are two types of iron—heme, which is found in animal products, and non-heme, which is derived from plants.

Select Sources of Iron
- Blackstrap molasses
- Chocolate and cocoa powder

- Dark leafy greens—beet greens, bok choy, collard greens, spinach, Swiss chard, and turnip greens
- Dried fruits—apples, apricots, dates, peaches, and raisins
- Fruits—grapefruit (canned), raspberries (frozen), strawberries (frozen), pineapple (canned), and watermelon
- Herbs and spices (dried)—anise seed, basil, bay leaf, black pepper, chervil, coriander, cumin seed, dill, marjoram, oregano, parsley, rosemary, spearmint, tarragon, thyme, and turmeric
- Juices—apricot nectar, grapefruit, pineapple, prune, and tomato
- Legumes—black-eyed peas, chickpeas, lentils, kidney beans, lima beans, navy beans, peas, pinto beans, soybeans, and white beans
- Nuts—almonds, cashews, and pistachios
- Seeds—pumpkin, sesame (and sesame butter/tahini), and squash
- Soy yogurt
- Tofu and tempeh
- Vegetables—broccoli, Brussels sprouts, green beans, and potatoes
- Whole grains—brown rice, bulgur, millet, oatmeal, and quinoa

MAGNESIUM

The fourth most abundant mineral in the body, magnesium is extremely important for muscle and nerve function. It also steadies the heart rhythm, supports a healthy immune system, and keeps bones strong.

Select Sources of Magnesium

- Dark leafy greens—collard greens, spinach (cooked), and Swiss chard
- Dried fruits—apricots, bananas, currants, dates, peaches, pears, prunes, and raisins
- Fruits—avocado, bananas, blackberries, raspberries, and watermelon
- Legumes—black-eyed peas, black lentils, kidney beans, lima beans, peanuts, pinto beans, and soybeans
- Nondairy milk—soy
- Nuts—almonds, black walnuts, Brazil nuts, cashews, and pine nuts
- Seeds—flax, pumpkin, sesame, and squash
- Tofu
- Vegetables—broccoli (raw), cabbage, okra (frozen), and potatoes
- Whole grains—brown rice and quinoa
- Whole-grain breads and cereal

MANGANESE

Small amounts of this trace element help us grow normally and maintain good health. Manganese plays a starring role in the metabolism of carbohydrates, amino acids, and cholesterol, and helps the body use key nutrients, like biotin, thiamin, choline, and vitamin C.

Select Sources of Manganese

- Blackstrap molasses
- Dark leafy greens—beet greens, collard greens, kale, mustard greens, romaine lettuce, spinach, Swiss chard, and turnip greens
- Dried fruits—figs

- Fruits—bananas, blackberries (frozen), grapes, pineapple, raspberries, strawberries, and wild blueberries
- Herbs and spices—black pepper, cardamom, chili powder, cinnamon, cloves, ginger, saffron, thyme, and turmeric
- Legumes—chickpeas, kidney beans, lentils, lima beans, navy beans, peanuts, peas, pigeon peas, pinto beans, soybeans, and split peas
- Maple syrup
- Nuts—almonds, cashews, hazelnuts, macadamia nuts, pecans, pine nuts, pistachios, and walnuts
- Seeds—flax, pumpkin, sesame (plus sesame butter/tahini), squash, and sunflower
- Tea
- Tempeh
- Vegetables—beets (raw), broccoli, Brussels sprouts, eggplant, garlic, squash, sundried tomatoes, and sweet potatoes
- Whole grains—amaranth, brown rice, buckwheat, bulgur, Kamut, oats, quinoa, spelt, teff, and wheat germ

MOLYBDENUM

One of the lesser-known minerals, molybdenum is a metallic element essential in trace amounts for help in metabolizing fats, carbohydrates, and amino acids and producing uric acid.

Select Sources of Molybdenum

- Legumes—black beans, chickpeas, green peas, kidney beans, lentils, lima beans, navy beans, and peanuts

- Nuts—almonds, cashews, and walnuts
- Seeds—sunflower
- Whole grains—barley, oats, rice, and wheat germ
- Whole-grain breads and cereals

PHOSPHOROUS

Helping to maintain strong healthy bones and teeth, phosphorous is also instrumental in supplying energy to the cells and helping the body absorb vitamins.

Select Sources of Phosphorous
- Legumes—beans, lentils, peanuts, peanut butter, and peas
- Nuts—almonds, cashews, Brazil nuts, pine nuts, pistachios, soybeans, and walnuts
- Seeds—flax, pumpkin, sesame, squash, and sunflower
- Vegetables—broccoli, corn, and garlic
- Whole-grain breads and cereals
- Whole grains—oat bran, rice bran, and wheat germ

POTASSIUM

Along with sodium, potassium helps regulate fluid in the body and aids in maintaining a regular heartbeat and low blood pressure. It's essential for the normal functioning of the heart, kidneys, muscles, nerves, and digestive systems.

Select Sources of Potassium
- Blackstrap molasses
- Dark chocolate
- Dark leafy greens—beet greens and spinach

- Dried fruits—apricots, dates, figs, prunes, and raisins
- Fruits—avocados, bananas, cantaloupe, dates, kiwifruit, orange, papaya, and watermelon
- Juices—carrot, orange, prune, and tomato
- Legumes—black-eyed peas, chickpeas, kidney beans, lentils, lima beans, peanuts, soybeans, split peas, and white beans
- Nuts—almonds, Brazil nuts, pine nuts, pistachios, and walnuts
- Seeds—poppy, sesame, and sunflower
- Vegetables—artichokes, broccoli, Brussels sprouts, carrots, mushrooms, parsnips, potatoes, spinach, sweet potatoes, tomatoes, and winter squash

SELENIUM

Selenium is an important antioxidant and cancer-prevention mineral, which protects against cellular damage from free radicals and helps to detoxify your systems.

Select Sources of Selenium
- Brewer's yeast
- Dark leafy greens—spinach, Swiss chard, and turnip greens
- Dried fruits—raisins
- Juices—grape and orange
- Nuts—Brazil nuts and walnuts
- Seeds—sunflower
- Vegetables—broccoli, cabbage, carrots, corn, garlic, mushrooms, and onions
- Whole grains—barley, brown rice, oats, and wheat germ

SODIUM

An electrolyte, sodium is necessary for muscle contraction and fluid maintenance, proper functioning of the circulatory system, and regulation of blood pressure. Please beware: Too much sodium in the diet poses health risks, such as hypertension and heart and kidney disease. Consume in moderation.

Select Sources of Sodium
- Fruits—Avocado
- Table salt (in moderation)
- Yeast extracts

SULFUR

Next to calcium and phosphorus, sulfur is the most abundant mineral in the body and is necessary for muscle, joint, and connective-tissue health, and is helpful in fighting the effects of aging and age-related illnesses, such as arthritis.

Select Sources of Sulfur
- Dark leafy greens—bok choy, collard greens, kale, mustard greens, and watercress
- Fruits—avocados and bananas
- Herbs—chives and parsley
- Legumes—peas and split peas
- Nuts—almonds, cashews, and walnuts
- Seeds—flax, sesame, and sunflower
- Tofu
- Vegetables—asparagus, broccoli, Brussels sprouts, cabbage, cauliflower, corn, garlic, green beans,

jicama, leeks, onions, radishes, shallots, sweet potatoes, tomatoes, and turnips
- Whole grains—oats and wheat germ

ZINC

An often-overlooked essential mineral, zinc is the most common mineral found in the body after iron. It plays a role in vision, taste, smell, wound healing, blood clotting, metabolism, reproduction, and many other functions.

Select Sources of Zinc
- Dark chocolate and cocoa powder
- Dark leafy greens—Swiss chard
- Dried fruits—bananas, currants, figs, peaches, and plums
- Fruits—apricots, avocado, blackberries, dates, longan berries, pomegranates, and raspberries
- Herbs—gingerroot (raw)
- Legumes—chickpeas, lima beans, black-eyed peas, kidney beans, peanuts, peas, pinto beans, and soybeans
- Miso
- Nutritional yeast
- Nuts—almonds, Brazil nuts, cashews, pecans, pistachios, and walnuts
- Seed butter—tahini (sesame butter)
- Seeds—chia, pumpkin, squash, and sunflower
- Tempeh
- Tofu
- Vegetables—asparagus, broccoli, Brussels sprouts, corn, garlic, green beans, hearts of palm, mush-

rooms, Napa cabbage, peas, pumpkin, and sun-dried tomatoes
- Whole grains—oatmeal and wheat germ
- Whole-grain fortified cereals

Omega-3 Fatty Acids

Omega-3 fatty acids boost heart health, lower triglycerides, and may help in the treatment and prevention of depression, Alzheimer's disease, strokes, some types of diabetes, and exercise-induced muscle inflammation.

Select Sources of Omega-3 Fatty Acids
- Dark leafy greens—kale, salad greens, and spinach
- Herbs (dried)—oregano, spearmint, and tarragon
- Herbs (fresh)—basil
- Legumes—soybeans
- Nuts—almonds and walnuts
- Seeds—chia, flax and flaxseed oil, hemp, and pumpkin
- Spices—ground cloves
- Tofu
- Vegetables—broccoli, Brussels sprouts, cabbage, and cauliflower

Protein

An important, life-sustaining nutrient composed of amino acids, protein helps build, maintain, and repair cells; supports the health of tissues, muscles, and organs; and is vital to nearly every function in the body, including metabolism, digestion, and the production of antibodies to fight infection.

Select Sources of Protein

- Dark, leafy greens—collard greens, kale, Swiss chard, and watercress
- Legumes—chickpeas, kidney beans, lentils, lima beans, peanuts and peanut butter, peas, pinto beans, soybeans, and split peas
- Nondairy milks
- Nuts—almonds and almond butter, cashews, pecans, pine nuts, and walnuts
- Seeds—pumpkin, sesame, and sunflower
- Tempeh, seitan, veggie burgers, and meat-substitute products (check label for fat content and dairy/egg ingredients)
- Tofu
- Vegetables—artichokes, asparagus, broccoli, Brussels sprouts, cauliflower, potatoes (with skin), squash (summer and winter), string beans, sweet corn, and sweet potatoes
- Whole grains—amaranth, brown rice, buckwheat groats, bulgur, millet, oatmeal, pearled barley, quinoa, rye berries, spelt berries, and teff

7

Great Grains

It's time to get your grain on. Our list of seventeen whole grains includes everything from the obvious (brown rice) to the obscure (teff). Each will add fun, variety, and texture to your daily menu. And unlike refined grains (read: white rice, white pasta, and white bread)—which have been stripped of their fiber and other healthful stuff—these pack a nutritional punch that's jammin' with protein, vitamins, minerals, and antioxidants.

Many of these grains can be found in your local supermarket (try the health-food or natural-food aisle). If not, explore the Internet. Last we looked, the mother of all online stores—Amazon (amazon.com)—carried every one of the grains listed below. Or check out other online grain suppliers like Pleasant Hill Grain (pleasanthillgrain.com) and Bob's Red Mill (bobsredmill.com).

Amaranth (gluten-free)

Considered a complete protein (meaning it contains all nine essential amino acids), this gluten-free grain is bursting with iron and calcium and has three times the fiber content of wheat. Serve it with a meal instead of rice or eat it as a hot cereal in the morning; we like it mixed with agave nectar, fresh fruit, and ground flaxseed.

To prepare: *Combine 1 cup amaranth with 2½ cups water and bring to a boil. Reduce heat, cover, and simmer for 20 minutes, until water is absorbed and amaranth is fluffy.*

Barley (contains gluten)

High in fiber, barley comes in two forms: hulled (the whole-grain form) and the easier-to-find pearled (bran layer removed). It's a versatile grain, great in soups, risotto, and salads, and is credited with lowering cholesterol.

To prepare: *Combine 1 cup barley with 3 cups water or vegetable broth and bring to a boil. Reduce heat, cover, and simmer until tender. (Approximate cooking times: pearled— 45 to 60 minutes; hulled—90 minutes.)*

Brown Rice (gluten-free)

Unlike white rice—which is brown rice that's been stripped of its nutrient-dense outer bran and germ layers—brown rice is brimming with vitamins, minerals, fiber, and fatty acids. You can find an array of varieties, including basmati, jasmine, long-grain (less starchy and ideal for pilaf-type dishes), and short-grain (makes for a stickier rice, suitable for risotto and sushi).

To prepare: *Combine 1 cup brown rice with 2¼ cups water or vegetable broth and bring to a boil. Reduce heat to low, cover, and simmer as follows: basmati—35 to 40 minutes; long- and short-grain—45 to 50 minutes. Fluff with a fork before serving. To trim cooking time, presoak brown rice for 30 minutes.*

Bulgur Wheat (contains gluten)

This rich, nutty-flavored grain is derived from wheat kernels that are steamed and toasted before they're cracked. Packed with folate, calcium, phosphorous, zinc, copper, iron, vitamin E, and many B vitamins, bulgur is one of our go-to rice substitutes, and makes delicious and nutritious salads, pilafs, and side dishes. Also tasty with stir-fries, curries, and stews.

To prepare: *Combine 1 cup bulgur wheat with 2 cups water or vegetable broth and bring to a boil. Reduce heat, cover, and simmer for 10 to 15 minutes. Fluff with a fork before serving.*

Cracked Wheat (contains gluten)

Made from crushed wheat kernels, this nutrient-dense grain is rich in fiber, folate, calcium, phosphorous, zinc, copper, iron, vitamin E, and many B vitamins. May be used in place of breadcrumbs, and as a side dish, pilaf, or salad (such as tabbouleh). Also makes a hearty breakfast cereal—top with almond milk, ground flaxseed, and fresh or dried fruit.

To prepare: *Combine 1 cup cracked wheat with 2 cups water or vegetable broth and bring to a boil. Reduce heat, cover, and simmer for 20 to 25 minutes. Fluff with a fork before serving.*

Farro (contains gluten)

Italian for emmer wheat, farro is loved for its roasted, nutty flavor and slightly crunchy texture. It's brimming with fiber, protein, magnesium, and B vitamins. Delicious in soups, as a side dish, and in salads.

To prepare: *Combine 1 cup farro with 2 cups water or vegetable broth and bring to a boil. Reduce heat, cover, and simmer for 25 to 40 minutes, until tender and water is absorbed.*

Kamut (contains gluten)

Kamut is the brand name for khorasan, an organically grown wheat that has ancient roots. Its large kernels have a slightly sweet, buttery flavor and are bursting with fiber and nutrients, including protein, vitamin E, B vitamins, and minerals. Great when served as a side dish or made into a salad with fresh chopped vegetables.

To prepare: *Combine 1 cup Kamut with 3 cups water or vegetable broth and bring to a boil. Reduce heat, cover, and simmer for about 1 hour, until grains are tender.*

Millet (gluten-free)

An excellent source of manganese, magnesium, and phosphorous, millet comes in two forms: pearled or hulled. Opt for hulled, which is the whole-grain, nutrient-intact variety. Mild tasting and versatile—with a light, ricelike texture—millet makes a delicious side dish or breakfast porridge.

To prepare: *Combine 1 cup millet with 1½ cups water or vegetable broth in a covered pot and bring to a boil. Reduce heat, cover, and simmer for 20 to 30 minutes. Fluff with a fork when done.*

Oats (gluten-free but often processed on equipment that processes gluten-containing grains; cross-contamination is possible; check labels)

This nutritional powerhouse is especially known for its cholesterol-lowering properties and is also high in protein and B vitamins. There are a number of varieties to choose from. All are derived from the same grain and are equally healthful—they're just cut and processed differently.

Oat groats—Whole oat grains with the outer bran layer left intact; only the hard outer hull is removed. Resembling brown rice, this grain has a sweet, nutty flavor and makes a delicious breakfast porridge.

To prepare: *Combine 1 cup oat groats with 3 cups water and bring to a boil. Reduce heat and simmer uncovered for 45 to 60 minutes, until tender.*

Steel-cut oats (also called Irish or pinhead oats)—Made by chopping oat groats with a steel blade to lessen cooking time. Since the whole grain remains intact, steel-cut oats are very nutritious.

To prepare: *Combine 1 cup steel-cut oats with 3 cups water and bring to a boil. Reduce heat and simmer uncovered for 20 to 40 minutes, stirring often, until tender. (Or, for a special, super-easy variation, see our recipe for Banana Overnight Oatmeal on page 161.)*

Rolled oats—Steamed groats that are flattened with a roller and dried, these come in three varieties: old-fashioned (or jumbo), quick cooking, and instant.

To prepare: *Combine 1 cup rolled oats with 2 cups water and bring to a boil. Reduce heat and simmer uncovered for up to 10 minutes (depending on variety), stirring often, until desired consistency is reached. (Also great served raw in our Perfect Cereal Bowl; see recipe on page 162.)*

Oat bran—The finely ground meal of the oat groats' bran layer, oat bran is high in fiber and makes a nutritious breakfast porridge (add nondairy milk and fresh fruit). Can also be added to other foods and is frequently used in baking.

To prepare: *Combine 1 cup oat bran with 2 cups water and bring to a boil. Reduce heat and simmer uncovered for 5 to 7 minutes, stirring often, until desired consistency is reached.*

Polenta (gluten-free)

An Italian staple once considered peasant food, polenta is typically made with coarsely ground yellow cornmeal, but there are also finely ground white and yellow varieties. It's gluten-free, low in carbs, high in nutrients—including vitamins A and C—and extremely versatile. Delicious with breakfast, lunch, or dinner, it's also excellent when grilled, added as a base to sauces, or layered into lasagna dishes.

To prepare: *Bring 4 cups water to a boil. Add 1 cup polenta, reduce heat, and cook over low heat until tender, 20 to 30 minutes. Stir frequently to avoid clumping. (In a hurry? Buy prepared polenta in a tube and just slice and roast.)*

Popcorn (gluten-free)

Corn, while considered a vegetable, is often dried into grains like grits, polenta, hominy, tortillas, and corn bread.

Plus, each kernel is a grain—and a nutritious one at that, bursting with protein and fiber. And who doesn't love to snack on popcorn? It's quick and easy to make.

To prepare: *Use a popcorn air popper or toss kernels into a brown paper bag and microwave for 3 to 4 minutes, until all kernels are popped. (Keep an ear out—when the popping stops, your snack is ready. Be careful the bag doesn't catch on fire, and open with caution—corn will be steaming hot.)*

For fun variations, check out our recipes for Cheesy Popcorn (page 152) and Kettle Corn (page 153).

Quinoa (gluten-free)

A snap to prepare, easy to digest, and loaded with nutrients—including magnesium, manganese, iron, copper, phosphorous, vitamin B_2, and other essential minerals—quinoa (pronounced KEEN-wah) is a complete protein (contains all nine essential amino acids) and boasts the highest protein content among all other grains. This gluten-free food comes in light brown, red, and black varieties and is delicious as a breakfast porridge (served with nondairy milk, fresh and dried fruits, and ground flaxseed), a side dish, and in salads.

To prepare: *Rinse well before cooking to remove the saponin, a natural, bitter-tasting coating that may remain after processing. Combine 2 cups water with 1 cup quinoa, cover pot, and bring to a boil. Reduce heat and simmer until the grain turns translucent and a thin white ring (the germ) forms around each grain, about 15 minutes. Fluff with a fork.*

Sorghum (gluten-free)

A gluten-free food, sorghum is a good source of protein, which can be eaten as a whole grain, in sorghum syrup, or as sorghum flour. Whole kernels resemble popcorn kernels that can be popped in much the same way for a super-easy, healthy snack. You can also eat it as a breakfast porridge or side dish.

To prepare: *Combine 4 cups water with 1 cup sorghum grains. Simmer for 25 to 40 minutes until soft.*

To pop: *Use a popcorn air popper or toss kernels in a brown paper bag and microwave until all kernels are popped (about 3 to 4 minutes, but keep an ear out; when you no longer hear popping, it's done).*

Spelt Berries (contain gluten)

An ancient grain and relative of wheat, spelt has a nutlike flavor and is brimming with nutrients, including heart-healthy niacin, manganese, vitamin B_2, thiamin, and copper. It is also known to help reduce cholesterol levels. Spelt berries make an excellent grain salad. Spelt flour is often used in baking. While low in gluten, spelt is not a gluten-free grain.

To prepare: *Combine 3½ cups water or vegetable broth with 1 cup spelt and bring to a boil. Reduce heat, cover, and simmer until tender, about 90 minutes.*

Teff (gluten-free)

The tiniest grain in the world—roughly the size of a poppy seed—teff means "lost" in Amharic, the official language of Ethiopia, where teff is widely harvested. Despite its diminutive size, the grain is packed with calcium, is an excellent source of vitamin C (not normally found in grains), and contains ample amounts of lysine, the amino acid essential for muscle repair. Many of

Ethiopia's elite long-distance runners and marathoners credit teff for their endurance and speed. The primary ingredient in *injera*, a spongy Ethiopian flatbread, teff also makes a delicious, nutrient-packed breakfast porridge and can be prepared as a polenta-like side dish.

To prepare: *Combine 3 cups water with 1 cup teff and bring to a boil. Reduce heat to low, cover, and cook until water is absorbed, about 20 minutes.*

Wheat berries (contain gluten)

With their chewy texture, nutty flavor, and high fiber content, wheat berries are the raw kernels of wheat whose inedible outer hull has been removed. They are the most unprocessed form of wheat, and therefore contain a host of nutrients, like protein, vitamin E, B vitamins, iron, phosphorous, folate, calcium, zinc, copper, and iron. Excellent in salads, as a breakfast porridge, a side dish, and when added to soups and stews.

To prepare: *Combine 3 cups water or vegetable broth with 1 cup wheat berries and bring to a boil. Reduce heat, cover, and simmer until berries are tender, 1½ to 2 hours.*

Wild rice (gluten-free)

A misnomer, wild rice is not rice at all, but the seed of an aquatic marsh grass indigenous to the Great Lakes region and Canada. It's loaded with health benefits, boasting nutrients like B vitamins, manganese, zinc, potassium, phosphorus, and magnesium, and contains twice the protein and fiber as brown rice. When cooked, wild rice has a rich, nutty flavor and chewy texture and comes in a variety of colors, ranging from medium brown to jet black. Try it in salads, stuffing, pilafs, and side dishes. We also love it in the morning as a break-fast "cereal," tossed with fresh and dried fruit, nuts, and almond milk.

To prepare: *Combine 3 cups water or vegetable broth and 1 cup wild rice and bring to a boil. Reduce heat, cover, and simmer until tender, 50 to 60 minutes. Fluff with a fork before serving.*

8

The Vegan Eat Sheet

A quick rundown of foods to indulge in and foods to avoid:

The Absolute No-Nos

Steer clear of these foods:

- Butter and margarine
- Cheese
- Eggs
- Fish and shellfish
- Foods containing dairy derivatives, such as casein and whey (see our section on reading labels, page 21)
- Lard
- Milk and cream
- Pork
- Poultry
- Red meat

The Only-If-You-Must List

To be ultra heart-healthy, you should consume these products in extreme moderation (avoid if you're a heart patient):

- Oils (corn, canola, olive, peanut, sesame, etc.)
- Sugar
- Vegan "butter"
- Vegan "cheese"
- Vegan "ice cream"

Consume in Moderation

These foods are healthy in smaller doses:

- Avocado (avoid if you're a heart patient)
- Nuts (avoid if you're a heart patient)
- Olives
- Peanut and other nut butters (avoid if you're a heart patient)
- Seeds and seed butters (avoid if you're a heart patient)
- Tofu
- Whole-grain breads (look for 100 percent whole grain)
- Whole-grain pastas

The Eat-As-Much-As-You-Want List

Go crazy with these foods:

- Beans and legumes—black beans, cannellini beans, chickpeas, Great Northern beans, kidney beans, lentils, lima beans, navy beans, pink beans, pinto beans, split peas, and so forth
- Fruits
- Grains (for a description of seventeen grains we love and how to prepare them, check out our Great Grains chapter on page 46)
- Vegetables

9

Vegan Replacements for Things You Love

Most of these items are available at your local grocery store or at health-oriented supermarket chains and health-food stores.

CAVEAT: If you're a heart patient, avoid foods containing fats, oils, coconut, and nuts.

Our Rating System:

* Eat only when desperate.

** Eat in moderation.

*** Go for it!

For BEEF OR CHICKEN STOCK

Use vegetable stock ***

For BUTTER
Use vegan buttery spreads *

For BUTTERMILK (in Recipes)
Use this combo: mix 1 cup soy or almond milk with 2 tablespoons lemon juice or white vinegar; let sit for 5 minutes. ***

For CHEESE
Use vegan cheese (beware: some soy cheeses contain milk derivatives, like whey or casein/caseinate) *

For COFFEE CREAMER
Use soy creamer ** or coconut-milk creamer **

For COTTAGE CHEESE (in Recipes)
Use mashed tofu (equivalent amount) **

For CREAM (in Alfredo Sauce)
Use cashew cream (see recipe, page 69) **

For CREAM CHEESE
Use tofu-based cream cheese *

For EGGS (in Recipes)
Use:

- 1 tablespoon ground flaxseed or flaxseed meal + 3 tablespoons warm water; let sit for 10 minutes = 1 egg ***
- powdered egg replacers (follow package directions) ***

For ICE CREAM/SORBET

Use:

- almond-, coconut-, and soy-milk-based "ice creams" and novelties **
- sorbets (avoid sherbets, as they contain milk products) **

For MAYONNAISE

Use vegan mayonnaise *

For MEAT

Sorry, there's no substitute that will trick you into thinking you're eating filet mignon. Meaty-textured foods like seitan ** (derived from wheat gluten), tempeh ** (made from slightly fermented soybeans), and other vegetable-protein-based meat alternatives, however, can do a pretty darn good job of satisfying your meat cravings.

For MILK

Use:

- almond milk ***
- almond-coconut milk **
- coconut milk ** (in carton, not can)
- hemp milk ***
- oat milk ***
- rice milk ***
- soy milk ***

For OIL (When Baking Sweets)

Use apple butter, applesauce, puréed banana, or pumpkin butter (conversion is 1 to 1) ***

For RICOTTA CHEESE (in Recipes)

Use mashed tofu (equivalent amount) **

See our recipe for Tofu Spinach Ricotta, page 156.

For SOUR CREAM

Use:

- vegan sour cream *
- plain soy yogurt **

For YOGURT

Use almond, coconut, or soy yogurt **

10

The Vegan Shopping List

Your Vegan Starter Set: Must-Have Staples for the Pantry and Fridge

We like to keep our kitchens well stocked with non-perishable basics. Making new recipes is so much easier when you've got most of the ingredients on hand. Here are our pantry and fridge staples:

CAVEAT: If you're a heart patient—or you're trying to lose weight—avoid avocados, chocolate, coconut, nuts, peanuts, and seeds. Everyone else should consume these in moderation.

Baking Ingredients
- Agave
- Baking powder
- Baking soda
- Brown sugar
- Cornmeal

- Dried cranberries
- Pure maple syrup
- Raisins
- Vanilla extract
- Unsweetened cocoa powder
- Whole-wheat flour (white whole-wheat and whole-wheat pastry are best choices for baking)

Beans and Legumes

- Dried lentils
- Beans of choice (many are available dried; we prefer canned for convenience)—black beans, cannellini beans, chickpeas/garbanzo beans, Great Northern beans, kidney beans, lima beans, navy beans, pink beans, white beans, and so forth

Breads

- Corn tortillas (oil free)
- Whole-grain bread (100 percent whole grains; that means no "wheat flour" unless it lists "whole wheat" in the ingredients)
- Whole-wheat breadcrumbs
- Whole-wheat tortillas (100 percent whole grains)

Canned Goods

- Apple butter (good for baking)
- Applesauce (good for baking)
- Light coconut milk
- Fruit jams or preserves (no sugar added)
- Marinara sauce—oil-free or low-fat (check labels for vegan)
- Seed butters—sunflower and sesame (tahini)
- Nut butters—almond, cashew, and peanut
- Silken light tofu (may be in Asian section)

- Tomatoes (plum)—chopped, crushed, and whole
- Tomato paste
- Vegetable stock (look for oil-free)

Cereals
- Oatmeal
  - We prefer standard rolled oats to eat raw in cereal
  - For baking, we use rolled, steel-cut Irish, and quick-cooking oats
- Various cereals—100 percent whole-grain with no added oils (we love Nature's Path Smart Bran and Ezekiel Cinnamon Raisin)

Condiments
- Balsamic vinegar
- Capers (in water)
- Chutneys (great to spice up wraps and rice and beans)
- Hot sauce (we love Cholula)
- Mustard—look for interesting variations like whole-grain or Dijon style, but check ingredients for dairy
- Olives (in water)
- Port, sherry, and/or vermouth
- Rice vinegar
- Salsa—standard tomato, as well as fun variations, like peach and mango
- Tamari and/or soy sauce
- White vinegar

"Dairy" (Can We Please Rename This Aisle?)
- Coffee creamer—soy or coconut

- Nondairy milk—almond, coconut, hemp, rice, or soy (our preference is unsweetened plain for savory cooking and vanilla flavored for desserts)
- Tofu—firm and silken (light, if possible)
- Vegan cheese (check the label to make sure it's casein/dairy-free)
- Yogurt—almond, coconut, or soy

Freezer Section
- Frozen edamame—great snack
- Frozen fruit—blueberries, mangos, peaches, and strawberries (perfect for pancakes and other treats)
- Frozen spinach—we use it so much in cooking
- Frozen vegetables—for desperate days when you can't get fresh
- Frozen-fruit bars
- Sorbet (note: avoid sherbets, which contain dairy products)
- Veggie burgers (make sure they're vegan—many contain eggs and/or cheese; find brands with as few ingredients as possible)

Grains and Pasta
Choose your faves. For more grain ideas and how to prepare them, see our Great Grains chapter on page 46.
- Amaranth
- Barley
- Brown rice—short-grain and precooked or quick cooking
- Bulgur
- Corn kernels for popping

- Farro
- Lasagna noodles—whole wheat, no boil
- Pasta—whole wheat or brown rice
- Quinoa

Herbs and Spices—Dried
- Allspice
- Basil
- Black pepper
- Cayenne
- Chili powder
- Cinnamon
- Cumin
- Curry powder
- Garlic powder
- Ginger, ground
- Nutmeg
- Oregano
- Paprika
- Red pepper flakes
- Rosemary
- Saffron
- Sage
- Sea salt
- Thyme

Indulgences
- Dark chocolate (not all is vegan; be sure to check)

Nuts—Raw or Dry Roasted
- Almonds
- Brazil nuts
- Cashews—raw (a must for cashew cream; recipe on page 69)

- Pecans
- Pine nuts
- Walnuts

Produce

- Fresh fruit—*tons*, in all colors; we especially love:
  - Apples, bananas (great to peel and freeze), berries, mangos, and melons
  - Lemons for cooking
- Fresh vegetables—*tons*, in all colors
  - We love bell peppers, broccoli, Brussels sprouts, cauliflower, green and yellow zucchini, sweet potatoes, and tomatoes
  - Be sure to get extra carrots, celery, garlic, ginger, and onions for freezing and cooking (see our Recipe Timesavers on page 69)
- Fresh herbs—basil, cilantro, oregano, parsley, rosemary, and thyme
- Dried fruits—apricots, cherries, cranberries, dates, figs, prunes, and raisins
- Salad and dark, leafy greens (buy pre-washed and organic when possible)—arugula, collard greens, endive, kale, mixed salad greens, radicchio, red-leaf lettuce, romaine lettuce, spinach, and watercress

Seeds

- Chia
- Flaxseed meal (ground flaxseed; store in fridge once opened); or buy whole flaxseeds and grind yourself
- Pumpkin
- Sesame
- Sunflower

Vitamins and Miscellaneous

You may want to buy these in your health-food store, although mainstream supermarket chains tend to carry them as well:

- Beano
- Nutritional yeast
- Vitamin B_{12}

- Pour 1 tablespoon cream into each section of ice cube tray and freeze; or freeze ¼-cup portions in small plastic resealable bags.
- Place frozen cubes in plastic zip bag in freezer.
- Use frozen in recipes as desired, adding a few extra minutes to recipe to defrost.

Celery

Use frozen in recipes as desired, adding a few extra minutes to recipe to defrost.

- Grab a few heads of celery, clean, remove ends, line up, and chop.
- Toss chopped celery into plastic zip bag and stash in freezer.
- To use: Bang bag on counter to loosen and remove what you need.
- Refreeze remainder.

Garlic

Use frozen in recipes as desired, adding a few extra minutes to recipe to defrost.

- Buy a tub of fresh, peeled garlic, chop in food processor, and freeze in ice cube trays (2 teaspoons garlic with ½ teaspoon water per section). When frozen, relocate to plastic zip bag and freeze.
  - *Or* freeze chopped garlic as is, without dividing into cubes. Toss into plastic bag and freeze.
- To use: Bang bag on counter to loosen and remove what you need.
- Refreeze remainder.

Ginger

Use frozen in recipes as desired, adding a few extra minutes to recipe to defrost.

Recipe Timesavers

Who Doesn't Love Shortcuts?

Here are some staples we use regularly that you can prepare quickly in advance—then just grab and go as needed:

Carrots

Use frozen in recipes as desired, adding a few extra minutes to recipe to defrost.

- Grab a large bag of baby peeled carrots and pulse in food processor, toss into plastic zip bag, and store in freezer.
- To use: Bang bag on counter to loosen and remove what you need.
- Refreeze remainder.

Cashew Cream

- Combine 1 cup raw cashews with 1 cup water.
- Purée mixture in food processor or blender and blend until texture is completely smooth.

- Buy a large head of ginger and peel. Snap small knobs for easy peeling of larger head.
- Chop in food processor and freeze in ice cube trays (2 teaspoons ginger with ½ teaspoon water per section). Relocate frozen cubes to plastic zip bag and store in freezer.
  - *Or* just freeze chopped ginger as is, without dividing into cubes. Toss into plastic bag and freeze.
- To use: Bang bag on counter to loosen and remove what you need.
- Refreeze remainder.

Onions

Use frozen in recipes as desired, adding a few extra minutes to recipe to defrost.

- Buy a bag of onions, chop in food processor, toss into plastic zip bag, and stow in freezer.
  - No-more-tears tip: Throw on some ski or swim goggles, and you'll remain dry-eyed while chopping.
- To use: Bang bag on counter to loosen and remove what you need.
- Refreeze remainder.

Veggies/Microwave

Use to quickly steam your veggies (or use the old-fashioned stovetop method, if you'd prefer).

- Place veggies in a microwave-safe bowl; add a few tablespoons of water.
- Cover with microwave-safe plastic wrap and cook on high in 3- to 5-minute increments.
- Be careful when removing plastic wrap to avoid a steam burn; I always open far side of bowl, away from my face.

Tools of the Trade

When Amy heads to the kitchen, she's armed with these must-have gadgets and gizmos:

Immersion/Stick Blender

If I were planning to live on a deserted island and could bring one kitchen tool, it would be the immersion blender. Of course, that's making the illogical assumption that electricity would be available. Petty details aside, my immersion blender is my under-$50 rock star! With it, I can purée soups in the pot, make Tofu Spinach Ricotta in minutes, and whip up decadent desserts in a flash. All without the sometimes messy cleanup demanded by food processors and blenders. Wow, I sound like a bad infomercial.

Heavy Dark Pot

Since all my cooking is oil-free, I prefer to use my heavy, old, worn-in pot, which helps "caramelize" onions and veggies as I sauté them. Some people prefer cast iron. Others may go for nonstick. Give your favorites a try and see what works best for you.

Large Colander/Strainer

I am seriously in love with my colander. If I were allowed a second item on that deserted island, this would be it. I must admit, for years I thought the colander was just another kitchen appliance. When I started to travel and cook in other kitchens, however, I pined for the large size and sturdy footing of my metallic baby. I use it daily to wash fruits and vegetables, as well as to drain pasta. My favorite trick is to fill it with raw baby spinach while cooking pasta. Then, I simply drain the pasta over the spinach and bam!—fresh wilted spinach and pasta.

Lisa has a couple of secret weapons, too . . .

Microplane

When shopping to stock my new kitchen recently, my sister (a great cook in her own right) insisted I buy a Microplane. I didn't even know what the heck it was, but now I do. It's become my go-to contraption for zesting lemons and limes, grating garlic and ginger, and shredding coconut. Most important, I use it to shave dark chocolate onto my "ice cream."

Rice Cooker

While living with a mom and her daughter in Costa Rica, I discovered the rice cooker—a staple in every Tico kitchen. The family and others in the community may not have had hot water, a phone, or more than dust for a floor, but they all had TVs and rice cookers—into which they threw rice, water, and lard. That made for some pretty awesome (albeit not-too-healthy) rice. I now skip the lard part, but I use the rice cooker for all my grains, including oatmeal. Just toss everything into the pot, push a button, and behold! Perfectly cooked grains that you don't have to watch, tend to, or clean up after when the water inevitably boils over the pot.

That's About It

Yup, except for a few other basics, like a good set of bowls, spoons, spatulas, cookie sheets, and other standard kitchen staples, this is all you need. Delicious vegan cooking is that easy!

13

The Twenty-One-Day Vegan Transformation

We Make the Vegan Transition a No-Brainer with Three Weeks' Worth of Vegan Menus

Ready to make the switch to vegan and concerned about what you'll eat over the next few weeks? Afraid you'll go hungry? Think you'll be bored? Worry no more. We've designed these daily menus to take the thinking out of mealtime while you adjust to your new lifestyle.

This is just a guide, so feel free to improvise, replace, mix, match, and refine depending on your mood and cravings. And if you don't feel like cooking, by all means eat out. Want more ideas? Visit our recipe section, beginning on page 92.

Note: If you're trying to shed pounds (or if you're a heart patient), please substitute all desserts, snacks, and avocados for fresh fruit or raw vegetables.

One of the great things about being vegan is that food doesn't spoil quickly. What you make on Monday will still be delicious on Thursday. So stash your extra muffins and bars, freeze your leftovers, double your recipes and save the surplus for another day . . . you get the picture. Once you dive in, you'll see how simple and fun it is to eat like a vegan. Bon appétit!

Day 1

BREAKFAST

Perfect Cereal Bowl (recipe on page 162) with almond milk and fresh berries

SNACK

Fresh fruit

LUNCH

If you eat at home: Simple Salad or Wrap of choice (recipes on pages 143–145)
If you go out: Salad bar with fresh veggies and beans, topped with low- or no-fat vinaigrette

SNACK

Soy, almond, or coconut yogurt and/or fresh fruit

DINNER

Whole-wheat pasta with Vodka Cream Sauce (recipe on page 131), Puttanesca Fresca (recipe on page 127), or jarred low-fat marinara, topped with ½ cup of cannellini beans and steamed broccoli

DESSERT

Cheesy Popcorn or Kettle Corn (recipes on pages 152 and 153), or oil-free popcorn of choice

Day 2

BREAKFAST

1 or 2 slices of toasted whole-grain bread topped with nut or apple butter and sliced bananas or apples

SNACK

Fresh fruit

LUNCH

If you eat at home: Bean-and-Grain Bowl (recipe on page 120)

If you go out: Hit Chipotle or other Mexican fast-food restaurant and order vegan-friendly menu items (see page 198 for ordering guidelines)

SNACK

Fresh vegetables and low-fat, oil-free hummus or dip of choice (recipes on pages 149–152 and 154)

DINNER

Italian Vegetable Terrine (recipe on page 108) or Eggplant "Parmesan" (recipe on page 94) and tossed salad, topped with dressing of choice (recipes on pages 146–149, or use store-bought, fat-free dressing)

DESSERT

Chia Pudding (recipe on page 177) and/or fresh fruit

Day 3

BREAKFAST

Power Breakfast Bar (recipe on page 163), vegan fruit-and-nut bar (see page 186 for suggestions), and/or fresh fruit

SNACK

Chia Pudding (recipe on page 177) or a handful of seeds of choice

LUNCH

Whole-wheat wrap with Baba Ganoush (recipe on page 150) or oil-free hummus and fresh vegetables

SNACK

Fresh fruit

DINNER

If you eat at home: Pad Thai (recipe on page 106)
If you go out: Head to your favorite Thai restaurant and order vegan-friendly dishes (request with no fish sauce or egg and with limited oil)

DESSERT

Baked Apple (recipe on page 169)

Day 4

BREAKFAST

Chocolate-Banana Dessert Shake (recipe on page 168)

SNACK

Power Breakfast Bar (recipe on page 163) or other bar of choice (see suggestions on page 186)

LUNCH

If you eat at home: Steamed vegetables and brown rice or other grain of choice

If you eat out: Head to a Chinese restaurant and order steamed vegetables and rice (request brown rice, if available)

SNACK

Fresh or dried fruit, seeds, or nuts

DINNER

Creamy Corn Chowder (recipe on page 134), salad, and dressing of choice (recipes on pages 146–149, or use store-bought fat-free dressing)

DESSERT

Apple Cobbler (recipe on page 170)

Day 5

BREAKFAST

Banana Overnight Oatmeal (recipe on page 161)

SNACK

Apple, plain or with peanut butter

LUNCH

Veggie burger with salsa and side salad with oil-free dressing of choice (recipes on pages 146–149, or use store-bought fat-free dressing)

SNACK

Power Breakfast Bar (recipe on page 163) or vegan fruit-and-nut bar of choice (see page 186 for suggestions) or fresh fruit

DINNER

Mushroom Risotto (recipe on page 95) and side salad with oil-free dressing of choice (recipes on pages 146–149, or use store-bought fat-free dressing)

DESSERT

Three squares of dark chocolate

Day 6

BREAKFAST

Vegan pancakes of choice (recipes on pages 157–159)

SNACK

Fresh fruit

LUNCH

Bean-and-Grain Bowl (recipe on page 120)

SNACK

Cheesy Popcorn or Kettle Corn (recipes on pages 152 and 153), or oil-free popcorn of choice and/or fruit

DINNER

Tomato-Basil Bisque (recipe on page 135) and side salad with oil-free dressing of choice (recipes on pages 146–149, or use store-bought fat-free dressing)

DESSERT

Frozen Banana Butter Treats (recipe on page 168) or store-bought frozen-fruit bar

Day 7

BREAKFAST

Breakfast Burritos (recipe on page 159)

SNACK

Nondairy yogurt and/or fresh fruit

LUNCH

Simple Salad or Wrap of choice (recipes on pages 143–145) or salad bar

SNACK

Fresh fruit

DINNER

Pizza of choice (recipes on pages 114–115) or order whole-wheat pizza, pasta sauce, no cheese, and add any vegetables you'd like

DESSERT

Chocolate Mousse (recipe on page 174) or three squares of dark chocolate

Day 8

BREAKFAST

1 or 2 slices of toasted whole-grain bread topped with nut or apple butter and sliced bananas or apples

SNACK

Crunchy Chickpeas (recipe on page 154)

LUNCH

Make a vegetable sandwich: whole-wheat bread, hummus, avocado, cucumber, lettuce, tomato, sprouts, etc.

SNACK

Fresh fruit

DINNER

Cassoulet (recipe on page 111) served with salad and oil-free dressing (recipes on pages 146–149, or use store-bought fat-free dressing)

DESSERT

Vegan muffin of choice (recipes on pages 165–167) and/or fresh fruit

Day 9

BREAKFAST

Apple-Cinnamon Muesli (recipe on page 161) or cereal of choice with fresh and/or dried fruit

SNACK

Roasted Red Pepper Tapenade (recipe on page 149) or hummus (buy oil-free or low-fat) with whole-wheat pita

LUNCH

Steamed vegetables with baked sweet potato

SNACK

Fresh fruit

DINNER

Chana Masala (Indian Chickpeas and Potatoes; recipe on page 105), Saag Paneer (Creamy Indian Spinach and Tofu; recipe on page 104), and brown rice or other grain of choice

DESSERT

Poached Pears (recipe on page 170) or fresh fruit

Day 10

BREAKFAST

Breakfast Parfait (recipe on page 163)

SNACK

Seeds and/or fresh fruit

LUNCH

Veggie burger with salsa and side salad with oil-free dressing of choice (recipes on pages 146–149, or use store-bought fat-free dressing)

SNACK

Vegan muffin of choice (recipes on pages 165–167) or buy your own and/or fresh fruit

DINNER

Pasta with Alfredo or sauce of choice (recipes on pages 127 and 130–131) with steamed spinach

DESSERT

Mango Sorbet (recipe on page 175) or store-bought sorbet or frozen-fruit bar

Day 11

BREAKFAST

Peach Pie Smoothie Bowl (recipe on page 176)

SNACK

Cheesy Popcorn or Kettle Corn (recipes on pages 152 and 153) and/or fresh fruit

LUNCH

Simple Salad or Wrap of choice (recipes on pages 143–145)

SNACK

Power Breakfast Bar (recipe on page 163), vegan fruit-and-nut bar of choice (see suggestions on page 186), or fresh fruit

DINNER

African Stew (recipe on page 100) with salad and oil-free dressing of choice (see recipes on pages 146, or buy your own)

DESSERT

Baked Apple (recipe on page 169) or fresh fruit

Day 12

BREAKFAST

Banana Overnight Oatmeal (recipe on page 161) or whole-grain cereal (see our recommendations, page 64)

SNACK

Fresh fruit

LUNCH
Simple Salad or Wrap of choice (recipes on pages 143–145)

SNACK
Fresh vegetables and oil-free or low-fat hummus or dip of choice (recipes on pages 149–152 and 154–155)

DINNER
Vegetable Fajitas (recipe on page 98) with brown rice and black beans

DESSERT
Frozen Banana Butter Treats (recipe on page 168)

Day 13

BREAKFAST
Breakfast Burritos (recipe on page 159)

SNACK
Fresh fruit

LUNCH
Steamed vegetables and brown rice or other grain of choice

SNACK
Seeds or popcorn and/or fresh fruit

DINNER
Tofu Parmesan (recipe on page 119), Thai Peanut Noodles (recipe on page 121), and steamed broccoli

DESSERT
Sorbet or frozen-fruit bar or fresh fruit

Day 14

BREAKFAST
Pancakes of choice (recipes on pages 157–159)

SNACK
Popcorn and/or fresh fruit

LUNCH
Veggie burger with side salad and oil-free dressing of choice (recipes on pages 146–149, or buy your own fat-free dressing)

SNACK
Fresh fruit or seeds

DINNER
Chilaquiles (recipe on page 107) with salad and oil-free dressing of choice (recipes on pages 146–149 or buy your own fat-free dressing)

DESSERT
Three squares of dark chocolate

Day 15

BREAKFAST
1 or 2 slices of toasted whole-grain bread topped with nut or apple butter and sliced bananas or apples

SNACK
Fresh fruit and/or seeds

LUNCH

Simple Salad or Wrap of choice (recipes on pages 143–145)

SNACK

Fresh vegetables and low-fat, oil-free hummus or dip of choice (recipes on pages 149–152 and 154–155)

DINNER

Tuscan Bean Stew (recipe on page 139) with brown rice or other grain of choice, plus salad and oil-free dressing (recipes on pages 146–149, or use store-bought fat-free dressing)

DESSERT

Poached Pears (recipe on page 170) or fresh fruit

Day 16

BREAKFAST

Breakfast Parfait (recipe on page 163)

SNACK

Crunchy Chickpeas (recipe on page 154) and/or fresh fruit

LUNCH

Simple Salad or Wrap of choice (recipes on pages 143–145) or load up at your favorite salad bar

SNACK

Fresh fruit

DINNER

Brazilian Vegetable Stew (recipe on page 99) with brown rice or other grain of choice

DESSERT

Sorbet or frozen-fruit bar

Day 17

BREAKFAST

Apple-Cinnamon Muesli (recipe on page 161)

SNACK

Yogurt or fresh fruit

LUNCH

Bean-and-Grain Bowl (recipe on page 120) or order at your favorite Mexican joint (for ordering suggestions, see page 198)

SNACK

Cheesy Popcorn or Kettle Corn (recipes on pages 152 and 153) or oil-free popcorn and/or fresh fruit

DINNER

Vegetable Lasagna (recipe on page 108) with salad and oil-free dressing of choice (recipes on pages 146–149, or use store-bought fat-free dressing)

DESSERT

Baked Apple (recipe on page 169) or fresh fruit

Day 18

BREAKFAST

Peach Pie Smoothie Bowl (recipe on page 176)

SNACK
Power Breakfast Bar (recipe on page 163), vegan fruit-and-nut bar of choice (see page 186 for suggestions), or fresh fruit

LUNCH
Simple Salad or Wrap of choice (recipes on pages 143–145) or visit you favorite salad bar

SNACK
Seeds and/or fruit

DINNER
Mujaddara (Lebanese Lentils; recipe on page 116) and salad with oil-free dressing of choice (recipes on pages 146–149, or use store-bought fat-free dressing)

DESSERT
Three squares of dark chocolate

Day 19

BREAKFAST
Banana Overnight Oatmeal (recipe on page 161)

SNACK
Fresh fruit

LUNCH
Steamed vegetables with brown rice or other grain of choice

SNACK
Fresh vegetables and oil-free, low-fat hummus or dip of choice (recipes on pages 149–152 and 154–155)

DINNER

Spinach Calzones (recipe on page 93) and salad with oil-free dressing of choice (recipes on page 66, or use store-bought fat-free dressing)

DESSERT

Cheesy Popcorn or Kettle Corn (recipes on pages 152 and 153) or oil-free popcorn of choice or fresh fruit

Day 20

BREAKFAST

Pancakes of choice (recipes on pages 157–159)

SNACK

Fresh fruit

LUNCH

Vegetable sandwich: whole-wheat bread, hummus, avocado, cucumber, lettuce, tomato, sprouts, etc.

SNACK

Cheesy Popcorn or Kettle Corn (recipes on pages 152 and 153) or oil-free popcorn of choice

DINNER

Pepper Vermouth "Pasta" (recipe on page 128) or pasta with sauce of choice (recipes on pages 127, 130–131) and salad with oil-free dressing (recipes on pages 146–149, or use store-bought fat-free dressing)

DESSERT

Chocolate Chip Biscotti (recipe on page 171) and/or fresh fruit

Day 21

BREAKFAST
Vegan muffin of choice (recipes on pages 165–167) with fresh fruit

SNACK
Fresh vegetables and low-fat, oil-free hummus or dip of choice (recipes on pages 149–152 and 154–155)

LUNCH
Veggie burger and side salad with oil-free dressing of choice (recipes on pages 146–149, or use store-bought fat-free dressing)

SNACK
Fresh fruit

DINNER
Paella (recipe on page 117) with vegetables and brown rice or other grain of choice

DESSERT
Chocolate Mousse (recipe on page 174) or chocolate squares or fresh fruit

No-Brainer Recipes

Three Steps . . . Twenty Minutes . . . 100 Percent Idiot-Proof

Here they are: Amy's special stash of vegan recipes, all a cinch to prepare and most requiring twenty minutes (or less) hands-on time. Even the sorriest cooks among us (raise your hand, Lisa) can master her easy, step-by-step formulas.

CAVEAT: If you're a heart patient, avoid recipes containing avocados, chocolate, coconut, nuts, peanuts, and seeds.

NOTE: Jar, can, and package sizes may vary slightly from what's listed in the recipes (for example, a 15-ounce can versus a 15.5-ounce can). These disparities are negligible and won't affect the outcome.

One-Dish Meals

Spinach Calzones

SERVES 4

My kids are super-picky eaters. I found that if I have them make their own calzones, they're much more likely to eat dinner without complaints (and perhaps they'll even be pleasant). I like to lay out the dough on the counter with a bowl of the spinach tofu blend, along with containers of other favorite veggies, like carrots, peppers, and edamame.

1 (14-ounce) box silken light tofu, drained

1 pound fresh baby spinach, steamed to wilt, and
   squeezed to remove excess water (or frozen,
   defrosted, and squeezed)

Dash nutmeg

1½ teaspoons salt

1½ pounds whole-wheat pizza dough

Whole-wheat flour, for dusting

Cornmeal for baking dish

Marinara, for serving (optional)

Preheat oven to 425°.

Blend tofu, spinach, nutmeg, and salt with a food processor, blender, or immersion blender, or mash together with a fork.

Divide dough into 4 pieces and roll each on a lightly floured surface in a circle, ⅛-inch thick. Place ¼ mixture in center of each dough circle, and fold in half, pressing edges to seal.

Dust a baking sheet with cornmeal, place calzones on sheet, and bake for 20 to 25 minutes or until light brown. If desired, serve with marinara.

Eggplant "Parmesan"
SERVES 4

The super-fried, gooey, oozing, cheesy version of this dish was always one of my favorites. I was shocked when I created this healthy vegan variation and my family loved it.

¾ cup whole-wheat breadcrumbs (4 slices whole-wheat toast ground in food processor)
¼ cup nutritional yeast
2 medium eggplants, thinly sliced (¼-inch thick)
1 (25-ounce) jar fat-free marinara sauce mixed with ½ cup water*

*OPTION: Mix in ¼ to ½ cup cashew cream; recipe on page 69.

Preheat oven to 375°.
Mix breadcrumbs with nutritional yeast.
Coat lasagna pan with sauce, then layer with eggplant, breadcrumb mixture, and sauce, repeating until all ingredients are used and ending with sauce.
Bake covered for 45 minutes to 1 hour. Serve hot.

Mushroom Risotto

SERVES 4

Did you know that classic risotto is often vegan if it contains vegetable stock or water instead of chicken stock? The cheese is usually an add-on after the dish is prepared. This would be awesome with chopped asparagus tips. Since I despise asparagus, however, I will stick to mushrooms. (Note from Lisa: Amy's crazy! I love asparagus and plan to toss it back in for a fun variation.)

2 cups vegetable stock

3 cloves garlic, finely chopped

1 cup brown short-grain or Arborio rice

1 pound sliced cremini/baby bella mushrooms, sliced (variation: use any other of your favorite mushrooms)

3 cups water

8 ounces fresh baby spinach or escarole

¾ cup white wine

2 teaspoons nutritional yeast

Salt and pepper, to taste

Heat ¼ inch of stock in a pan over medium heat. Add garlic and rice and cook for 3 minutes. Add more stock to barely cover rice and add mushrooms.

Stir continuously, and as liquid absorbs, add stock ½ cup at a time. After stock is used up, add water ½ cup at a time. Add spinach to wilt. When rice is al dente (about 35 to 40 minutes), add wine. Stir in nutritional yeast.

Cook 5 more minutes and add salt and pepper, to taste.

Chiles Rellenos

SERVES 4 TO 8

Why fry when you can bake? It's healthier for you and tastes just as good. In this recipe, tofu makes a great stand-in for the cheese. With all of these awesome flavors, you won't miss the artery-clogging fats in the original version.

1 (14-ounce) box firm light tofu, drained
1 pound fresh baby spinach, steamed to wilt, and
    squeezed to remove excess water (or use
    frozen, defrosted and squeezed)
1 teaspoon salt
1 teaspoon cumin powder
1 tablespoon chili powder
1½ cups cooked brown rice
8 poblano chile peppers, tops, cores, and seeds
    removed
½ cup whole-wheat breadcrumbs
½ cup cornmeal
½ cup unsweetened plain almond milk
1 cup tomato sauce

Preheat oven to 425°.

Blend tofu, spinach, and spices in a blender until smooth.

Combine mixture with rice and stuff inside poblano chile peppers.

Mix breadcrumbs and cornmeal in a bowl. Roll each pepper in almond milk to moisten and then into breadcrumb-cornmeal mixture to coat. Place peppers in a baking dish and cover loosely with foil. Bake for 40 minutes. Uncover and bake an additional 10 minutes. Top with warmed tomato sauce to serve.

Vegetable Fried Rice

SERVES 4

Prior to my going vegan, I frequently attempted—and failed miserably at—concocting a good version of fried rice. When creating a recipe for this book, I learned an important lesson: less is more.

1 cup chopped onion

8 ounces sliced mushrooms

2 cups broccoli florets

1 cup bean sprouts

1 teaspoon salt, or to taste

1½ cups brown rice, cooked

1 tablespoon tamari or soy sauce, or to taste

In a heavy dry pan on medium heat, cook onions until brown. If onions begin to stick, add water, ¼ cup at a time.

Add mushrooms, broccoli, bean sprouts, and salt and sauté until broccoli is tender (5 to 10 minutes).

Add rice and tamari and cook until heated.

Stuffed Portobello Mushrooms

SERVES 4

These passed muster with my wonderful yet meat-eating sister-in-law. She even asked for the recipe. Need I say more?

¾ cup quinoa, rinsed

2 cloves garlic, chopped

2 cups chopped kale

1½ cups vegetable stock

2 tablespoons chopped fresh basil

1 tablespoon tomato paste

4 large portobello mushroom caps, stems removed

1 tablespoon nutritional yeast

Preheat oven to 375°.

Place quinoa, garlic, kale, and vegetable stock in a medium pot. Cover and simmer for 15 minutes until liquid is absorbed.

Stir in basil and tomato paste. Scoop ¼ mixture on top of each mushroom cap.

Place stuffed mushrooms on a baking sheet and sprinkle each with nutritional yeast. Bake for 35 to 40 minutes. Remove from oven and serve hot.

Vegetable Fajitas
SERVES 4

I dreamed up this recipe in college when I proposed to feed my friends in exchange for prep and kitchen cleanup. Good deal, especially since I am a messy cook.

½ cup agave nectar or pure maple syrup

¼ cup tamari or soy sauce

1 large onion, sliced in strips

1 red bell pepper, cored, seeded, and sliced

1 green bell pepper, cored, seeded, and sliced

2 green zucchinis, sliced

1 cup sliced mushrooms

4 whole-wheat tortillas (burrito size)

Whisk agave nectar and tamari together until well blended.

Place onions, peppers, zucchini, and mushrooms in agave sauce to marinate for 10 to 15 minutes.

In a heavy dry pan, sauté vegetables and sauce on high heat, stirring regularly until vegetables are tender and caramelized, about 10 minutes. If there's excess liquid, remove it from the pan and save; you can add it back in later, if desired. Roll mixture inside tortillas like burritos. *¡Buen provecho!*

Brazilian Vegetable Stew
SERVES 4 TO 6

I tasted a version of this stew on a trip to Florida, and it reminded me of my friend Shannon's recipe. Since then, I've made so many changes that I'm not sure if it's even Brazilian anymore. Oh well, the name just sounds too good to pass up.

1 cup chopped onion

2 cloves garlic, chopped

1 tablespoon finely chopped ginger

1 (28-ounce) can diced plum tomatoes, undrained

1 large sweet potato, peeled and diced

1 large green zucchini, diced

1 large yellow zucchini, diced

1 medium eggplant, diced

½ teaspoon salt

½ teaspoon saffron (soaked in 2 tablespoons hot
   water to bloom)
¾ cup canned light coconut milk; shake can before
   opening (for a lower-fat option, substitute
   ¾ cup plain almond milk mixed with ¾ teaspoon
   coconut extract)

In a heavy dry pan, sauté onions over medium heat
until light brown. Add garlic and ginger and cook for 3
minutes. If ingredients begin to stick, add water, ¼ cup
at a time.

Add tomatoes and sweet potatoes and cook for
5 minutes.

Add remaining ingredients, except coconut milk, and
cook covered over medium heat until vegetables are tender, about 10 to 15 minutes. Add coconut milk and heat
through. If desired, serve over brown rice or other grain.

African Stew

SERVES 4 TO 6

Super rich, thick, and hearty. Great for a snowy night.

½ cup onion, diced
3 cloves garlic, minced
1 teaspoon ginger, minced
1 (28-ounce) can crushed tomatoes
1 large sweet potato, peeled and diced (about
   1½ cups)
1 teaspoon salt
½ teaspoon cayenne
1 (15-ounce) can chickpeas/garbanzo beans,
   drained

¼ cup peanut butter
½ cup water (optional)
1 pound fresh baby spinach (optional)

In a heavy dry pan, sauté onions over medium heat until light brown. Add garlic and ginger and cook for 3 minutes. If ingredients begin to stick, add water, ¼ cup at a time.

Add tomatoes, sweet potatoes, salt, and cayenne and cook, covered, over medium heat for 15 minutes.

Add chickpeas and peanut butter and heat through. Add water if thinner stew is desired. Serve as is or, if desired, over fresh baby spinach.

Stuffed Peppers

SERVES 4 TO 6

This is a perfect substitute for the classic version. I actually think these are more flavorful than their meat-engorged cousins.

1 cup chopped onions
2 cloves garlic, chopped
2 cups sliced mushrooms
½ teaspoon salt
¼ teaspoon black pepper
2 cups water
1 cup quinoa, rinsed
¼ cup tomato paste
4 large bell peppers, tops cut off and seeds removed
1 cup marinara sauce (optional)

Preheat oven to 425°.

In a heavy dry pan, sauté onions over medium heat until light brown. Add garlic, mushrooms, salt, and pepper and cook 2 more minutes. If ingredients begin to stick, add water, ¼ cup at a time.

Add remaining ingredients, except peppers and marinara. Cover and cook on low for 15 to 20 minutes, until liquid is absorbed.

Divide mixture into 4 parts and stuff each pepper (cut a thin slice off the bottom of each pepper to help it stand upright in pan). Place peppers in a baking dish and cook covered for 30 minutes. Top with marinara, if desired.

Shepherd's Pie

SERVES 4

Perfect for a Sunday-night family dinner. Serve with a salad to lighten it up.

1 cup chopped onion
½ cup chopped carrots
½ cup chopped celery
2 cloves garlic, chopped
1 teaspoon dried rosemary
¼ teaspoon black pepper
2 tablespoons tomato paste
1 cup dried green or brown lentils, rinsed and
   sorted for debris
3 cups water
1 teaspoon salt, divided
2 large Idaho potatoes, peeled, cut, and microwaved
   in bowl covered with water until tender, or
     2 cups Perfect Mashed Potatoes (page 125)
¼ cup unsweetened plain almond milk

Preheat oven to 425°.

In a heavy dry pan, sauté onions, carrots, and celery over medium heat until vegetables begin to soften. Add garlic, rosemary, and pepper, and cook 2 more minutes. If ingredients begin to stick, add water, ¼ cup at a time.

Add tomato paste, lentils, and water and simmer for 20 to 30 minutes, or until lentils are tender. Add ½ teaspoon salt. Place stew in a small casserole dish.

Mash potatoes with almond milk and remaining ½ teaspoon salt (omit if using Perfect Mashed Potatoes) and spoon over lentil mixture. Bake uncovered for 10 to 15 minutes. Serve and enjoy.

Macaroni and Cheese

SERVES 4

For four long mac-and-cheese-deprived years, I tried to create a delicious substitute for the great American classic. Eureka! I got it!

1 pound whole-wheat macaroni pasta
    (or other shaped pasta)
2½ cups fresh cauliflower florets
⅔ cup sweet potatoes, peeled and diced
1¾ cups plus 1 tablespoon unsweetened
    plain almond milk
2½ teaspoons salt
1¼ teaspoons garlic powder
2½ tablespoons nutritional yeast
¾ cup whole-wheat breadcrumbs (4 slices
    whole-wheat toast ground in food processor)

Preheat oven to 425°.

Cook pasta according to package directions, drain, and set aside.

Steam cauliflower and sweet potato in a pot or microwave in 5-minute increments until tender.

With a food processor, blender, or immersion blender, purée cauliflower, sweet potato, almond milk, salt, garlic powder, and nutritional yeast until smooth, and stir sauce into pasta.

Place in a baking dish, top with breadcrumbs, and bake uncovered for 15 minutes. Enjoy piping hot.

Saag Paneer (Creamy Indian Spinach and Tofu)

SERVES 4

My husband and I adore Indian food and were crushed when we realized that most vegetarian Indian dishes contain ghee (clarified butter). No wonder we were leaving our favorite Indian joint with stomachaches! This spinach dish combines just the right amount of spice with the rich creamy spinach. I like to serve this with Chana Masala (see recipe, page 105), brown rice, mango chutney, and a side of warmed whole-wheat pita bread.

2½ cups chopped onion

6 cloves garlic, minced

2 teaspoons grated fresh ginger

½ teaspoon ground pepper

½ teaspoon cayenne pepper

½ teaspoon garam masala (spice blend)

½ teaspoon cumin

1 (28-ounce) can chopped tomatoes, undrained

1 pound washed baby spinach

1 (14-ounce) box firm tofu, drained and cubed

2 cups cooked brown rice (optional)

In a heavy dry pan over medium heat, sauté onions until light brown. Add garlic, ginger, and spices and cook 2 more minutes. If ingredients begin to stick, add water, ¼ cup at a time.

Add tomatoes and cook on low for 15 minutes. Add spinach and cook until fully wilted.

Purée with an immersion blender, blender, or food processor. Add tofu and heat through. Serve over brown rice, if desired.

Chana Masala (Indian Chickpeas and Potatoes)

SERVES 4

A Finnish woman in love with Indian cuisine? That's Lisa's mom, Alicia—who's traveled to India and loves the country's aromatic, spicy food. She's a big fan of this dish. It's one of my all-time favorites, too. Enjoy with Saag Paneer (see recipe on page 104).

1 onion, finely chopped

2 teaspoons grated fresh ginger

2 cloves garlic, chopped

2 cups peeled and cubed potatoes

1 cup water

3 tablespoons tomato paste

1 tablespoon curry powder

1 teaspoon cumin

½ teaspoon salt

1 (16-ounce) can chickpeas/garbanzo beans,
   drained and rinsed

¾ cup coconut milk; shake can before opening (for
   a lower-fat option, substitute ¾ cup plain almond
   milk mixed with ¾ teaspoon coconut extract)

In a heavy dry pan, sauté onions over medium heat until light brown. Add ginger and garlic and cook 3 more minutes. If ingredients begin to stick, add water, ¼ cup at a time.

Add potatoes, water, tomato paste, curry powder, cumin, and salt and cook over medium heat.

When potatoes are just done, add chickpeas and coconut milk and heat through.

Pad Thai

SERVES 4

A super-simple version of the classic Thai noodle dish that's to-die-for delicious.

2–3 tablespoons packed sugar

3 tablespoons fresh lime juice

4 tablespoons tamari or soy sauce

3 cloves garlic, minced

3 green onions, chopped

1 (16-ounce) package Thai rice noodles, cooked
   according to package instructions

3 cups broccoli florets, steamed in microwave for
   2–4 minutes

¼ cup chopped fresh cilantro
¼ cup chopped peanuts or other nuts (optional)

In a large saucepan, combine sugar, lime juice, tamari, garlic, and scallions and simmer over medium heat for 5 minutes.

Toss noodles with sauce and broccoli. Top with cilantro and add peanuts, if desired.

Chilaquiles
Great for breakfast, too!
SERVES 6

While living in San Diego, my husband and I would devour this traditional Mexican dish on a regular basis. It's made with sausage, cheese, and corn tortillas, and fried. What could be better? As I was reminiscing about our days in Southern California, I fondly recalled the yummy chilaquiles we loved so much. Maybe I've just forgotten the taste of sausage and cheese, but this version rocks my world.

1 (14-ounce) box silken light tofu
8 small corn tortillas, cut into strips
1 cup green or red chile sauce or tomato sauce
1 cup fresh chopped tomatoes

Drain tofu, mash with fork, and set aside.

In a heavy dry pan, place tortilla strips over medium heat and top with sauce and tomatoes. Stir occasionally until almost all sauce is absorbed.

Stir in tofu and heat through. Serve hot and enjoy.

Italian Vegetable Terrine

SERVES 4

Make this in advance. It's so easy, and the taste improves each day.

2 red bell peppers, cored, seeded, and sliced into
   ½-inch strips

1 red onion, peeled and sliced

1 (25-ounce) jar fat-free marinara sauce

1 tube prepared polenta (sliced ¾-inch thick)

1 large eggplant, thinly sliced (¼-inch thick)

2 green zucchinis, thinly sliced (¼-inch thick)

2 yellow zucchinis, thinly sliced (¼-inch thick)

¼ cup nutritional yeast

Preheat oven to 425°.

Roast peppers and onions on a cookie sheet covered with foil for 30 minutes, turning once.

Reduce oven temperature to 375°.

Coat a 9 x 13-inch baking dish with sauce, then layer in half of the veggies and top with half the remaining sauce and polenta. Repeat with remaining ingredients, ending with sauce. Top with nutritional yeast. Bake covered for 45 minutes. Enjoy.

Vegetable Lasagna

SERVES 4 TO 6

Another dish that my kids eat with gusto (if I make their half without zucchini).

1 (14-ounce) box silken light tofu, drained
2 cups chopped cauliflower, steamed in microwave
    in 5-minute increments or until very tender
1 teaspoon salt
1 (25-ounce) jar oil-free tomato sauce mixed with
    ½ cup water*
1 (9-ounce) box whole-wheat lasagna, uncooked
1 green zucchini, thinly sliced
1 yellow zucchini, thinly sliced

*OPTION: I like to mix in ¼ to ½ cup cashew cream
instead of the water; recipe on page 69.

Preheat oven to 425°.

Blend tofu, cauliflower, and salt with an immersion
blender, blender, or food processor until creamy, or
mash with a fork.

Coat bottom of a 9 x 13-inch lasagna pan with sauce,
then layer pasta, sauce, tofu blend, and zucchini. Repeat,
ending with pasta and sauce. Bake covered for 45 to
55 minutes. Cut into squares and serve.

Baked Ziti/Spaghetti Pie
SERVES 4

*Tired of serving my kids plain old pasta, I just threw it
in a baking dish, added some healthy stuff, and voilà!
Instant, new, good-for-you dinner disguised as a treat.*

1 (14-ounce) box silken light tofu, drained
1 pound fresh baby spinach, steamed to wilt,
    and squeezed to remove excess water
    (or frozen, defrosted and squeezed)

2 teaspoons salt
1 (1-pound) box whole-wheat pasta, cooked
    al dente
1 (25-ounce) jar oil-free marinara
2 tablespoons nutritional yeast

Preheat oven to 425°.

In a medium bowl, blend tofu, spinach, and salt with an immersion blender, blender, or food processor until creamy, or whisk with a fork.

In a 9 x 13-inch lasagna pan, mix pasta with tofu-spinach blend and sauce. Top with nutritional yeast.

Bake uncovered for 15 minutes. Remove from oven and serve hot.

Mushroom Farro Pasta

SERVES 4

When I was growing up, my nana would make a classic Jewish dish called kasha varnishkes. *This updated version is healthy, delicious—and perhaps even a bit chic.*

1 cup farro
2¼ cups vegetable stock
2 cups onion, chopped
1 pound mushrooms, sliced
1 teaspoon salt
½ teaspoon black pepper
8 ounces (½ box) whole-wheat cut pasta
    (such as fusilli or bowties), cooked to package
    directions

In a medium saucepan, combine farro and vegetable stock, cover, and simmer 20 to 30 minutes until liquid is absorbed. Farro will remain a bit crunchy.

In a separate heavy dry pan, sauté onions over medium heat until light brown. Add mushrooms, salt, and pepper. If ingredients begin to stick, add water, ¼ cup at a time.

Combine farro, onion mixture, and pasta to serve. Enjoy warm or cold.

Cassoulet

SERVES 4

I learned to love the art of making French cuisine from a fabulous cook—my mom. I believe that even she could become a vegan devotee after tasting this hearty classic—sans le boeuf!

1 pound cremini or baby bella mushrooms, sliced

½ pound portobello mushrooms, cubed

½ pound shitake mushrooms, chopped

1½ cups pearl onions, peeled (fresh or frozen)

3 cloves garlic, minced

1 (15-ounce) can diced tomatoes, drained

1 teaspoon dried thyme

1 tablespoon fresh rosemary, chopped, or 1 teaspoon dried

1 teaspoon salt

½ teaspoon black pepper

2 (15-ounce) cans cannellini or Great Northern beans, drained and rinsed

½ cup port wine

½ cup whole-wheat breadcrumbs

Preheat oven to 475°.

In a heavy dry pan, sauté mushrooms and onions over medium-high heat for 10 minutes. Add garlic and cook another 2 minutes. If ingredients begin to stick, add water, ¼ cup at a time.

Add tomatoes, thyme, rosemary, salt, and pepper and cook covered for 30 minutes. Add beans and wine and cook 10 more minutes.

Transfer all to a casserole pan, top with breadcrumbs, and bake for 10 minutes. Remove from oven and serve.

Spicy Thai String Beans and Tofu
SERVES 4

This knock-your-socks-off dish is quick and easy to make. Adjust the spiciness to taste by adding or subtracting curry paste. Thai curry paste generally comes in a small jar and can be found in most major supermarkets in the Asian foods section. Try the red or green variety.

4 cloves garlic, chopped

¼ cup vegetable stock

½ pound fresh, trimmed string beans

2 tablespoons Thai red curry paste

2 tablespoons tomato paste

1 cup canned light coconut milk; shake can before
    opening (for a lower-fat option, substitute
      1 cup plain almond milk mixed with 1 teaspoon
      coconut extract)

1 (14-ounce) box cubed, firm, low-fat tofu, drained

Salt, to taste

2 cups brown rice (optional)

In a heavy dry pan, sauté garlic in vegetable stock over medium heat for 2 minutes.

Add remaining ingredients and cook on medium heat until green beans are heated.

Serve over brown rice or other grain of choice.

Falafel
SERVES 4

Some things taste better when doused in grease (french fries, for example). But this is one of those times you can say, why fry? This baked version is just as good and vice-free. Eat it alone or in a sandwich. My friend (and assistant) Meg and her family keep begging for more.

1 (15-ounce) can chickpeas/garbanzo beans, drained
⅓ cup cilantro leaves (or parsley for cilantro haters)
⅓ cup chopped red onions
2 garlic cloves
½ teaspoon salt
¼ teaspoon black pepper
¼ teaspoon cayenne pepper
1 teaspoon ground cumin
¼ teaspoon baking powder
½ tablespoon fresh lemon juice
Chickpea or other flour (if needed; see below)
Water (if needed; see below)
Lettuce, tomato, and whole-grain pita (optional)

Preheat oven to 400°.

Combine all ingredients (except water and flour) in a food processor. Process until you can form mixture into balls. Add flour if too wet and water if too dry, 2 tablespoons at a time.

Form 1-inch balls and place on a cookie sheet. Flatten each ball slightly.

Bake for 15 minutes, flipping patties halfway through. Eat alone or with lettuce, tomato, and whole-grain pita.

Veggie Pizza

SERVES 4

My husband used to complain that the only thing he missed as a vegan was a really good pizza. Now he has nothing to yammer about. (Although I speculate that he may find something else, non-food related.)

1 (14-ounce) box silken light tofu, drained
1 pound fresh spinach, steamed to wilt and squeezed to remove excess water (or frozen, defrosted, and squeezed)
Dash nutmeg
1 teaspoon salt
Cornmeal, for dusting
Whole-wheat flour, for dusting
1 pound whole-wheat pizza dough
2 cups pizza sauce
Your favorite vegetable toppings (peppers, tomatoes, mushrooms, broccoli, broccoli rabe, onions; the more, the better!)

Preheat oven to 425°.

Blend tofu, spinach, nutmeg, and salt with an immersion blender, blender, or food processor, or mix with a fork.

Dust a baking sheet with cornmeal.

Roll dough on a flour-dusted surface into a large circle or rectangle to fit baking pan and top with sauce, tofu mixture, and vegetables of choice. Bake for 25 minutes or until crust is lightly browned.

BBQ Tofu Pizza

SERVES 4

This is a great twist on traditional pizza that's perfect for summer suppers. By the way, I've heard you can grill pizza on the barbecue. If I ever figure that one out, this is the one I will try. Meanwhile, let's stick with the oven.

1 pound whole-wheat pizza dough

⅓ cup barbeque sauce plus 2 tablespoons,
    for drizzle

1 small red onion, thinly sliced

½ (14-ounce) box firm tofu, drained and crumbled
    or diced into ½-inch cubes

¼ cup cherry tomatoes, cut in half

Cornmeal, for dusting

Whole-wheat flour, for dusting

3 tablespoons fresh cilantro, chopped

Preheat oven to 425°.

Dust a baking pan with cornmeal.

Roll dough on flour-dusted surface into a large circle or rectangle to fit baking pan and top with sauce, onion, tofu, and tomatoes. Drizzle 2 tablespoons sauce over toppings.

Bake for 20 minutes or until crust is lightly browned. Sprinkle with cilantro and serve.

Mujaddara (Lebanese Lentils)

SERVES 4

Not only is this delicious and nutritious, but it's fun to say (moo-juh-dra). Great warm or cold, this makes for awesome leftovers.

2 cups onion, sliced

2 cloves fresh garlic, chopped

1 cup dried green or brown lentils, rinsed and
    sorted for debris

2 cups water

1 teaspoon salt

1 cup cooked brown rice or quinoa

1 cup chopped fresh tomatoes

¼ cup chopped parsley

SPICE BLEND

(Make extra and save to add flair to other dishes.)

¼ teaspoon ground cinnamon

½ teaspoon black pepper

½ teaspoon paprika

½ teaspoon allspice

½ teaspoon cumin

In a heavy dry pan, sauté onions over medium heat until light brown. Add garlic and spice blend, and cook 2 more minutes. If ingredients begin to stick, add water, ¼ cup at a time.

Add lentils and water. Simmer for 20 to 30 minutes (cooking time may vary depending on age of lentils). Stir in salt and cook 2 more minutes.

Stir in rice. Remove from heat and top with chopped tomatoes and parsley.

Three-Bean Chili with Smoked Tempeh

SERVES 8

This ultra-easy chili is a crowd pleaser—perfect for winter nights and Super Bowl parties.

1 large onion, sliced

1 red or green bell pepper, cored, seeded, and diced

1 (28-ounce) can chopped plum tomatoes, undrained

1 (15-ounce) can black beans, undrained

1 (15-ounce) can Great Northern or cannellini beans, undrained

1 (15-ounce) can kidney beans, undrained

½ cup smoked (or any other) tempeh, chopped

2 cloves garlic, chopped

2 teaspoons salt

1 tablespoon chili powder

In a heavy dry pan, sauté onions and peppers over medium heat until onions begin to brown. If ingredients begin to stick, add water, ¼ cup at a time.

Add all remaining ingredients and cook covered on medium-low heat for 1 hour. Serve or save for a rainy day (it gets better after a few days in the fridge).

Paella

SERVES 6 TO 8

Prior to going vegan, I made the classic chicken-sausage-seafood paella for my husband as a treat. It

was an excellent tool for scoring well-needed "brownie points." Well, guess what? It still works in this veg-anized version. Here you go, honey!

1 cup chopped onion

3 cloves garlic, chopped

1 red bell pepper, cored, seeded, and sliced

1 green zucchini, cut into chunks

1 yellow zucchini, cut into chunks

1 small eggplant, cut into chunks

½ cup finely chopped fresh string beans

4 cups vegetable stock

3 cups short-grain brown or Arborio rice

1 (28-ounce) can plum tomatoes, undrained

2 teaspoons saffron (soaked in 4 tablespoons hot water to bloom)

2 teaspoons salt

4–6 cups water

In a heavy dry pan, sauté onion, garlic, pepper, zucchini, squash, eggplant, and string beans over medium heat for 10 minutes or until vegetables begin to soften. If ingredients start to stick, add water, ¼ cup at a time.

Cover vegetables with ¼ inch of vegetable stock and add rice. Crackle rice for 3 minutes. Add tomatoes, saffron mixture, and salt. Stir continuously, and as liquid absorbs, add stock, ½ cup at a time. When stock is used up, add water ½ cup at a time. Stir regularly.

Continue to add water until rice is al dente, about 35 to 40 minutes. Spoon into bowls and enjoy.

Tofu Parmesan

SERVES 4

This awesomely simple and outrageously delicious rec-
ipe was given to me by a great friend and fabulous chef.
Thanks, Uncle Pete!

½ cup nutritional yeast

2 tablespoons tamari or soy sauce

1 (14-ounce) box firm tofu, drained and sliced
    ¾-inch thick

1 pound spinach, steamed

Preheat oven to 425°.

Place nutritional yeast and tamari on separate plates.
Dip each slice of tofu in tamari then nutritional yeast,
turning to coat both sides. Reserve extra tamari and yeast.

Place on cookie sheet and roast 10 to 12 minutes until
top is light golden brown. Toss spinach with remaining
tamari and nutritional yeast and place tofu on top to serve.

Stuffed Cabbage

SERVES 4 TO 6

Always use caution when attempting to re-create your
mother in-law's famous holiday recipe. I love this adap-
tation, and it passes her approval, too (doesn't it, Joan?
Joan?).

1 cup onion, chopped

½ cup carrots, chopped

½ cup celery, chopped

1 pound mushrooms, sliced

2 cloves garlic, chopped

1 teaspoon salt

1 (15-ounce) can red beans, drained or 1½ cups
cooked lentils

1 large head of cabbage, scored around core and
microwaved for 2 to 4 minutes to soften

1½ cups sauerkraut, drained

1 (28-ounce) can crushed tomatoes, undrained

½ cup brown sugar

Preheat oven to 325°.

In a heavy dry pan, sauté onion over medium heat until light brown. Add carrots, celery, mushrooms, garlic, and salt and cook 10 more minutes. If ingredients begin to stick, add water, ¼ cup at a time. Stir in beans and set aside.

Carefully remove leaves from cabbage, trying to keep whole. Retrieve the best 8 leaves. If the leaves are too hard to remove, microwave for another 1 to 2 minutes.

Stuff each leaf with ¾ cup to 1 cup of bean mixture. Fold ends on top to form package and place seam side down in a baking dish. Top with sauerkraut and tomatoes and sprinkle with brown sugar. Bake covered for 2 to 2½ hours, basting every 30 minutes. Serve hot.

Bean-and-Grain Bowl

SERVES 2

I could eat this every day for lunch. Feel free to change it up and have fun. Experiment with marinara, soy sauce, or nutritional yeast. Maybe add some steamed broccoli. Or put various toppings on the table and let your family members or guests make their own bowls.

2 cups field greens, baby spinach, kale, or greens
    of choice
1½ cups cooked brown rice, quinoa, or your grain
    of choice
1 (15-ounce) can black beans or any beans of
    choice, drained
1 cup salsa—tomato, mango, or any other variety

Heat beans and grains separately.
In 2 bowls, layer greens, rice, and beans. Top with salsa.

Thai Peanut Noodles
SERVES 4 TO 6

When Lisa's dad, Ed, plucked a bunch of cucumbers from his garden, he decided to whip up a refreshing salad that was admittedly peculiar sounding: cukes, noodles, and peanut butter. When she told me how delicious and refreshing it was, I conjured up this easy-to-make rendition. Ed, you're a great guy with great taste buds!

⅓ cup tamari or soy sauce
⅓ cup rice vinegar
2 tablespoons lime juice
2 tablespoons brown sugar
2 cloves garlic, minced
2 tablespoons creamy peanut butter or nut butter
    of choice, plus additional, to taste

½ teaspoon hot sauce (choose your fave; we love Cholula)

1 (10-ounce) package buckwheat soba noodles, cooked according to package directions; drained and rinsed

2 large cucumbers, peeled, cut in half, seeds scooped out, and sliced

½ cup chopped peanuts (or other nuts)

½ cup chopped fresh cilantro

In a small pot, combine tamari, rice vinegar, lime juice, sugar, garlic, peanut butter, and hot sauce and simmer for 10 minutes.

In a serving bowl, toss sauce with noodles, cucumbers, nuts, and cilantro. Serve at room temperature or chilled.

Perfect Sides

These make excellent accompaniments to your meals, or they can be prepared as light main dishes.

Potato-Black Bean Salad

SERVES 6 TO 8 AS A SIDE DISH

This summer, my husband, Ken, nagged (did I say that?) me to whip up a good potato salad. I avoided the task due to my fear of a potentially blah mayonnaise-free version. (What's potato salad without mayonnaise?) Well, I finally gave in and was thrilled with the result.

2 pounds red potatoes, cut lengthwise and sliced
   into ½-inch pieces, steamed in microwave in
   3-minute increments or until just tender; do
   not overcook
½ cup white vinegar
2 tablespoons sugar
2 teaspoons salt
1 teaspoon prepared mustard
1 (15-ounce) can black beans, drained and rinsed
1 red bell pepper, cored and diced
½ cup chopped green onion

Whisk together vinegar, sugar, salt, and mustard until well blended.

Toss potatoes, vinegar blend, and remaining ingredients. Let stand 15 to 20 minutes, tossing regularly before serving. For best flavor, store overnight in refrigerator.

Oven-Roasted Root Vegetables

SERVES 4 AS A MAIN COURSE OR 8 AS A SIDE DISH

This was inspired by my dear friend Jamie. Actually, I think my whole career was inspired by her.

1 large sweet potato, peeled and cut into 1-inch
   chunks
2 beets, peeled, rinsed, and cut into 1-inch chunks
2 parsnips, peeled and cut into 1-inch chunks
12 baby carrots
1 large white potato, peeled and cut into 1-inch
   chunks

1 cup pearl onions, peeled (fresh or frozen)
2 tablespoons fresh rosemary, chopped, or 2 tea-
   spoons dried
1 teaspoon dried and ground sage
1–2 teaspoons salt, to taste

Preheat oven to 425°.
In a large bowl, toss all ingredients.
Lay on a baking sheet and roast for 45 minutes or until all vegetables are tender, shuffling/tossing vegetables every 15 minutes.

Oven-Roasted Tomatoes

SERVES 4 AS A SIDE DISH

So good and a cinch to make. Great to bring as a side to a dinner party.

4 large tomatoes—lay on side and cut in half
2 teaspoons nutritional yeast

Preheat oven to 425°.
Lay tomato halves on a baking sheet, skin side down. Sprinkle each with ¼ teaspoon nutritional yeast.
Roast for 15 minutes on top shelf of oven.

BBQ Kale

SERVES 4 AS A MAIN COURSE OR 8 AS A SIDE DISH

I think this was the first vegan recipe I ever created, and it's always a hit at barbeques. We often enjoy it as a main course served over polenta or a baked sweet potato.

2 cups vegetable stock

1 pound kale, chopped

1 (16-ounce) can baked beans (fat-free, vegetarian)

2 red bell peppers, cored, seeded, and chopped

4 ears corn (raw, cut kernels off cob) or 1
    (15-ounce) can corn, drained

2 (15-ounce) cans black beans, drained and
    rinsed

Combine all ingredients in a large pot. Cook over medium-low heat for 30 to 40 minutes.

Serve alone or over polenta or a baked sweet potato.

Perfect Mashed Potatoes

SERVES 4 TO 6 AS A SIDE DISH

This prize-winning recipe was created by my fabulous consultant Susan (she actually did win a 4-H award for her non-vegan version).

4 Idaho potatoes, peeled and chopped

½ cup (approximately) unsweetened plain
    almond milk

Salt and black pepper, to taste

Boil or microwave potatoes (covered with water, 5-minute increments) until very tender, then drain.

With a hand mixer, whip potatoes until no chunks remain (rub through fingers to test).

Slowly add almond milk, 2 tablespoons at a time, until desired moisture is achieved. Add salt and pepper to taste.

Sauce on Top

Pick your top and pick your bottom. Then mix and match the endless variations.

BOTTOMS:

Baked potato

Baked sweet potato

Brown rice

Farro

Gluten-free pasta

Polenta, sliced and
    roasted

Quinoa

Spaghetti squash

Steamed kale

Steamed spinach

Whole-grain pasta

TOPS:

And they say "She's just a writer, she can't cook." This recipe was inspired by my coauthor and pastaholic, Lisa—an awesome chef in her own right.

Alfredo Sauce

SERVES 4

¾ cup raw cashews
¾ cup water
3–4 cloves garlic, minced
4 tablespoons nutritional yeast
1 teaspoon salt
Black pepper, to taste
¼ cup to 1 cup water

In a blender or food processor, purée cashews and water until smooth.

In a heavy dry pan, cook garlic over low heat for 3 minutes. Add cashew cream, nutritional yeast, salt, pepper, and ¼ cup water.

Heat thoroughly, adding more water if sauce is too thick. Toss with "bottom" of choice and serve immediately.

Puttanesca Fresca

SERVES 4

I concocted—and trashed—so many awful versions of this dish that I almost gave up. (Maybe it's because I hate olives and capers. Hmmm . . .) But my puttanesca-loving friends encouraged me to press on. Thank goodness! I actually adore my raw version—the flavors aren't quite as biting as the original, and the fresh tomatoes are a delightful touch.

1 cup chopped fresh tomatoes

1 cup chopped pitted olives (your favorite)

2–3 tablespoons capers, undrained

Toss all ingredients together with "bottom" of choice, and serve warm or cold.

Pepper Vermouth "Pasta"
SERVES 4

I literally make this once a week for dinner. Sometimes I use the vermouth or sherry and other times I use leftover red or white wine. Occasionally I even add a bit of vegan sausage.

1 large onion, sliced

3 bell peppers (any color), cored, seeded, and
   sliced

2 cups cherry tomatoes, sliced

A pinch of red pepper flakes (optional)

¾ cup sweet vermouth or sherry (or red or
   white wine)

In a heavy dry pan, sauté onions and peppers over medium heat until onions begin to brown. If ingredients begin to stick, add water, ¼ cup at a time.

Add tomatoes and red pepper flakes, if using, and cook for 5 more minutes.

Add vermouth to pan. If using pasta or spaghetti squash, add these to pan. Cook for 2 minutes on high, then serve.

Artichoke "Pasta" Salad
SERVES 4

I created this dish one day when I was invited to a summer potluck and forgot to shop in advance. I just looked in my pantry, glanced at my vegetable basket, tossed, and went.

1 (15-ounce) can chopped water-packed arti-
    chokes, undrained
1 (15-ounce) can of white cannellini or Great
    Northern beans, drained
2–3 tablespoons capers, undrained (optional)
1 cup halved cherry tomatoes
¼ teaspoon salt
Pinch ground black pepper

In a large bowl, mix together all ingredients.
Toss with pasta or "bottom" of your choice and serve warm or cold.

Ratatouille
SERVES 4 TO 6

I have been making this recipe since my pre-vegan college days. No revisions were necessary.

1 cup chopped onion
4 cloves garlic, minced
1 (28-ounce) can chopped plum tomatoes, undrained
1 medium green zucchini, diced

1 medium yellow zucchini, diced

1 small eggplant, diced

2 red peppers, cored and diced

1 teaspoon salt

1 teaspoon dried thyme

½ teaspoon dried rosemary

½ cup sweet red wine

In a heavy dry pan, sauté onions over medium heat until light brown. Add garlic and cook 2 more minutes. If ingredients begin to stick, add water, ¼ cup at a time.

Add remaining ingredients through rosemary and cook covered over medium-low heat, for 40 minutes.

Add wine, and cook for 3 to 5 minutes. Serve alone or with "bottom" of choice.

Port Mushroom Sauce

SERVES 4

This unbelievable sauce is my latest favorite. I adore it so much that I lick the pot after serving—when nobody's looking.

¾ cup raw cashews

¾ cup water

¾ cup pearl onions, peeled (fresh or frozen)

½ pound shitake mushrooms

¾–1½ cups port

Salt and pepper to taste

In a blender, purée cashews and water until smooth.

In a heavy dry pan, sauté onions and mushrooms over medium-high heat for 10 minutes. If ingredients begin to stick, add water, ¼ cup at a time. Add port and simmer for 2 to 3 minutes, stirring constantly.

Lower heat to low and add cashew cream. Add salt and pepper to taste. Serve over "bottom" of choice.

Vodka Cream Sauce

SERVES 4

Confessions of a vegan chef: one night, I was trying to throw together a quick, nutritious dinner for my kids and—gasp!—my vegetable drawer was empty. I did, however, have a stash of cashew cream in the freezer. Since I always have pasta and marinara sauce on hand, this yummy dish was born. Note: I didn't use much vodka in my kids' version and I made sure to render it (boil it off) fully—otherwise, the evening would have been a bit, well, livelier.

¼ cup raw cashews
¼ cup water
1 (24-ounce) jar fat-free marinara or pasta sauce
2 tablespoons vodka

In a blender or food processor, purée cashews and water until smooth.

Stir cashew cream into pasta sauce in pot over medium heat.

Add vodka and simmer for 2 to 3 minutes, stirring constantly. Serve over "bottom" of choice.

Hearty Soups and Stews

Warm the soul and keep it simple.

Curried Butternut Squash Soup

MAKES 8 CUPS OR 4 BOWLS

I grew up believing that making soup was a huge, hours-long endeavor: "First you start with a whole chicken . . ." Yikes! This super-easy recipe was my first experience with the simplicity of making a great pot of soup.

4 cups butternut squash,* cooked
2 cups vegetable stock
2 cups unsweetened plain almond milk
1 teaspoon curry powder
½ teaspoon salt

*Try to buy fresh, pre-cut chunks and microwave in a bowl with ½ cup of water. If pre-cut is not available, then cut squash in half, scoop out seeds, and cut into chunks. Microwave in 5-minute increments until squash is very tender. Or to save time, buy frozen cubes and defrost.

Blend all ingredients with an immersion blender, blender, or food processor until creamy.

Place in a medium pot and heat to warm through.

Distribute evenly into cups or bowls and enjoy.

Southwest Black-Bean Soup

MAKES 4 CUPS OR 2 BOWLS

My clients love this heartwarming soup. I've created a super-simple version that's fast, easy, and amazingly delicious.

2 (15-ounce) cans black beans, undrained
1 (15-ounce) can whole corn, undrained
¼ cup chopped onion
1–2 cloves garlic, peeled
1 teaspoon chili powder
½ teaspoon sea salt

Blend all ingredients together with a food processor, blender, or immersion blender until creamy (with small bits of corn and bean visible).

Cook over medium-low heat for 20 to 30 minutes to let the flavors meld.

Distribute evenly into cups or bowls and enjoy.

Posole Soup

MAKES 6 CUPS OR 4 BOWLS

I used to love this soup in my PV (pre-vegan) days. I was thrilled to come up with an easy substitute for the pork-laden original.

1 cup chopped onion
¾ cup chopped carrots
1 red bell pepper, cored, seeded, and chopped

3 cloves garlic, minced

½ teaspoon cumin

½ teaspoon salt

1½ teaspoons chili powder

1 (15-ounce) can crushed tomatoes

3 cups vegetable broth

1 (15-ounce) can hominy, drained

Fresh cilantro, chopped (optional)

In a heavy dry pan, sauté onions over medium heat until brown. Add carrots, peppers, garlic, cumin, salt, and chili powder and continue to cook, 3 to 4 minutes. If ingredients begin to stick, add water, ¼ cup at a time.

Add tomatoes, broth, and hominy and simmer covered 30 to 40 minutes.

Distribute evenly into cups or bowls, top with cilantro (if desired), and serve.

Creamy Corn Chowder

MAKES 6 CUPS OR 4 BOWLS

This is hands-down the best soup I make. Grown-ups and kids alike clamor for seconds.

½ cup chopped onion

½ cup red bell peppers, cored, seeded, and
    chopped

¼ cup diced celery

1 cup peeled, diced potatoes

½ teaspoon salt

2 (15-ounce) cans corn, drained with liquid
    reserved

Water

½ cup unsweetened plain almond milk

¼ teaspoon cayenne pepper (optional)

In a heavy dry pan, sauté onions, peppers, and celery over medium heat until onions begin to brown. If ingredients begin to stick, add water, ¼ cup at a time.

Add potatoes, salt, and all liquid from canned corn. Add water until potatoes are just covered. Cover and cook until potatoes are just tender, about 15 minutes, and set aside.

In a blender or food processor, mix half of the corn and the almond milk and blend until creamy. Pour over onion-potato mixture, add remaining corn, and heat until warm. Distribute evenly into bowls, add cayenne (if desired), and serve.

Tomato-Basil Bisque

MAKES 4 CUPS OR 2 BOWLS

My kids' favorite. So good, so quick, and so loved, you may not want to share this recipe. Oh no, I actually just did.

½ cup raw cashews

½ cup water

1 (24-ounce) jar fat-free pasta or marinara sauce

¼ cup chopped basil

In a blender or food processor, purée cashews and water until smooth.

Stir cashew cream into pasta sauce over medium heat. Add basil and distribute evenly into bowls and serve.

White Miso Noodle Soup

MAKES 8 CUPS OR 4 BOWLS

I keep all the ingredients for this in my house all winter. It makes such a perfect quick meal and warms from head to toe.

8 cups water
½ cup mellow white miso paste, or more, to
    taste
1¼ teaspoons salt (optional)
1 pound pre-cut mixed Asian vegetables (fresh or
    frozen)
8 ounces buckwheat soba noodles, cooked
    according to package directions; drained
    and rinsed

In a large pot, combine water, miso, and salt over medium heat and stir to dissolve.

Add vegetables to soup and cook 5 minutes.

Add cooked noodles to soup. Distribute evenly into bowls and serve immediately.

Cream of Broccoli Soup

MAKES 6 CUPS OR 4 BOWLS

Although I love this version of cream of broccoli soup, the recipe almost didn't make the book. You see, I've revised the dang thing so many times that I lost count. After thinking I'd perfected the recipe a few years ago, I made a batch for sixty clients—and hated it so much that I tossed the entire vat. Trial and error finally paid off. Now, this is one of my new faves.

1 cup chopped onion

½ cup chopped carrots

½ cup chopped celery

3 cloves garlic, chopped

1 teaspoon salt

1 small head broccoli, chopped (around 2 cups) and steamed in microwave in 3-minute increments until tender

½ head cauliflower, chopped (around 2 cups) and steamed in microwave in 5-minute increments until tender

2 medium potatoes, peeled and cubed (around 2½ cups), steamed in microwave in 5-minute increments until tender

2 cups vegetable broth

1 cup unsweetened plain almond milk

Sweet vermouth (optional)

In a heavy dry pan, sauté onions, carrots, and celery over medium heat until vegetables are tender. Add garlic and salt and cook 2 more minutes. If ingredients begin to stick, add water, ¼ cup at a time.

Add onion mixture and all remaining ingredients except sweet vermouth to a food processor and blend until smooth.

Heat and serve. For an adult-only option, top each bowl with 1 to 2 teaspoons of vermouth.

Pasta e Fagioli

MAKES 8 CUPS OR 4 BOWLS

A super-hearty soup that everyone loves, and can double as a meal.

1 cup chopped yellow onions

½ cup chopped carrots

½ cup chopped celery

1 teaspoon salt

¼ teaspoon crushed red pepper flakes (optional)

4 cloves garlic, minced

2 (15-ounce) cans Great Northern or cannellini beans, drained, divided, liquid reserved

1 (28-ounce) can Italian plum tomatoes, chopped with liquid

1 teaspoon agave nectar

2 cups cooked pasta of choice (use leftovers, if available)

¼ cup fresh basil, chopped

In a large heavy pot, sauté onions over medium heat until light brown. Add carrots, celery, salt, red pepper flakes, and garlic and cook 2 more minutes. If ingredients begin to stick, add water, ¼ cup at a time.

Separately, purée 1 can of beans with the drained liquid of both cans. Add bean purée, 1 can whole beans, tomatoes, and agave nectar to pot. Simmer covered for 20 minutes.

Add pasta and heat through. Place stew in bowls, top with fresh basil, and serve.

Creamy Gazpacho

MAKES 4 CUPS OR 2 BOWLS

My dear friend Nikki served me this awesome creamy gazpacho. I was never a fan of the popular chunky version, but I adore this one.

1 slice whole-wheat bread
¾ pound (3–4 cups) ripe tomatoes, quartered
1 red bell pepper, cored, seeded, and quartered
½ medium red onion, peeled and quartered
½ cucumber, peeled
¼–½ cup tomato juice (½ cup for thinner soup)
1–2 garlic cloves
1 teaspoon sherry vinegar (or red wine vinegar)
¾ teaspoon salt
½ teaspoon ground black pepper

Place all ingredients in a food processor and blend on high until smooth.

Distribute evenly into bowls and serve cold or at room temperature.

Tuscan Bean Stew

MAKES 6 CUPS OR 4 BOWLS

I remember riding my bike through Tuscany with my amazing girlfriends when I tried the authentic version of the area's famous soup, La Ribolitta. I actually prefer my version, which uses beans to thicken the stew instead of bread.

1 cup chopped yellow onions

½ cup chopped carrots

½ cup chopped celery

1 (28-ounce) can chopped Italian plum tomatoes
with liquid

4 cloves garlic, minced

1 teaspoon salt

½ teaspoon crushed red pepper flakes

2 (15-ounce) cans Great Northern or cannellini
beans, drained, divided, and liquid reserved

2 cups coarsely chopped or shredded savoy
cabbage

½ cup chopped fresh basil leaves

¼ cup chopped smoked tempeh (optional)

In a heavy dry pot, sauté onions, carrots, and celery over medium heat until vegetables are tender. Add tomatoes, garlic, salt, and red pepper flakes and simmer for 20 minutes. If ingredients begin to stick, add water, ¼ cup at a time.

In a separate bowl, purée 1 can of beans with the drained liquid of both cans and set aside.

Add cabbage to vegetable mixture until cabbage wilts, then add whole beans, bean purée, basil, and tempeh. Heat through. Distribute evenly into cups or bowls and serve.

Mediterranean Lentil Soup

MAKES FOUR 1-CUP SERVINGS

My favorite Mediterranean restaurant would serve a version of this soup with crispy pita chips floating on top. Toast some u   bread, crumble, and give it a try.

1 cup chopped yellow onion
½ cup chopped carrots
½ cup chopped celery
4 cloves garlic, minced
¼ teaspoon allspice
1 teaspoon cumin
½ teaspoon ground cinnamon
¼ teaspoon ground black pepper
1½ cups dried red lentils, rinsed and sorted for debris
5 cups water
1 teaspoon salt, or to taste
2 tablespoons fresh lemon juice
⅓ cup parsley, chopped, for garnish

In a heavy dry pot, sauté onions, carrots, and celery on medium heat until onions begin to brown. Add garlic and spices (except salt), and cook 2 more minutes. If ingredients begin to stick, add water, ¼ cup at a time.

Add lentils and water and simmer until lentils are very tender, 20 to 30 minutes (cooking time may vary depending on age of lentils).

Stir in salt and lemon juice and heat through. Serve in bowls topped with chopped parsley and pita crisps, if desired.

Pumpkin-Quinoa Soup

MAKES 6 CUPS OR 4 BOWLS

I admit that I was a bit skeptical when I first tried to make this soup. But ultimately, I was blown away by its warm, delicious flavor. And the miracle is, I got it right the first time! (Not a common occurrence, as my family will attest.)

4 cups water
¾ cup quinoa, rinsed
1 cup chopped onion
½ cup chopped carrots
½ cup chopped celery
1 clove garlic, minced
1½ teaspoons salt
1 teaspoon curry powder
1 teaspoon dried crushed thyme
1½ cups canned pumpkin (not pumpkin pie filling)
1¼ cups light coconut milk; shake can before
    opening (for a lower-fat option, substitute
    1¼ cups plain almond milk mixed with
    1¼ teaspoons coconut extract)

In a soup pot, bring 1½ cups water and quinoa to a boil. Simmer covered until liquid is absorbed, about 15 minutes.

In a separate heavy dry pan, sauté onions, carrots, and celery over medium heat until vegetables are tender. Add garlic, salt, and spices and cook 5 more minutes. If ingredients begin to stick, add water, ¼ cup at a time.

With an immersion blender, blender, or food processor, blend onion mixture, pumpkin, remaining water, and coconut milk. Add to quinoa pot and heat through. Distribute evenly in cups or bowls and serve.

Simple Salads and Wraps

Make easy meals in a bowl or toss ingredients inside a whole-wheat tortilla for grab-and-go goodness. Pick your favorites, mix and match!

Fiesta Salad/Wrap

I love to make this wrap when I'm on the run but need a hearty meal.

CHOOSE YOUR FAVORITE INGREDIENTS:

Greens of choice (romaine, red-leaf lettuce, baby spinach, mixed greens, etc.)

Olives

Salsa

Black beans

Green onions

Raw peppers

Roasted peppers (roast at 425° for 45 minutes)

Roasted garlic (roast at 425° for 45 minutes in aluminum foil pouch)

Pan-roasted onions (sauté sliced onions in heavy dry pan over medium heat)

Hominy

Fresh mango, chopped

Pumpkin seeds

Chili powder (pinch)

Cumin (pinch)

Top with Mango Vinaigrette (recipe on page 146).

Asian Salad/Wrap

I could eat this every day.

CHOOSE YOUR FAVORITES:

Greens of choice (romaine, red-leaf lettuce, baby
spinach, mixed greens, etc.)

Broccoli slaw

Firm tofu, cubed

Steamed broccoli

Brown rice

Buckwheat noodles, chilled

Mandarin oranges (canned)

Slivered almonds

Water chestnuts (canned)

Baby corn (canned)

Edamame (cooked and shelled)

Top with Ginger-Soy Vinaigrette (recipe on page 147).

Caesar Feast

Great to make in advance for picnics and parties.

CHOOSE YOUR FAVORITES:

Romaine lettuce

Chopped tomatoes

Whole-wheat croutons (cube whole-wheat bread,
toss with nutritional yeast, and bake at 400°
until crispy)

Capers

Cannellini beans
Chopped cucumbers
Sunflower seeds
Roasted peppers (roast at 425° for 45 minutes)
Roasted garlic (roast at 425° for 45 minutes in
    aluminum foil pouch)

Top with Caesar dressing (recipe on page 146).

Harvest Salad/Wrap

Hearty enough for lunch or dinner on a chilly fall day.

CHOOSE YOUR FAVORITES:
Greens of choice (romaine, red-leaf lettuce,
    baby spinach, mixed greens, etc.)
Roasted butternut squash, cubed (roast at 425°
    until tender, 30 to 40 minutes)
Dried cranberries
Chopped walnuts
Roasted garlic (roast at 425° for 45 minutes in
    aluminum foil pouch)
Quinoa (cooked according to package directions)
Avocado
Hummus

Top with balsamic or Roasted Pepper–Balsamic Vinaigrette (recipe on page 148).

Oil-Free Salad Dressings/Marinades

They'll rock your greens!

Mango Vinaigrette/Marinade

MAKES 1 CUP; ABOUT 8 SERVINGS

So easy. Try substituting different salsas and vinegars for variety.

1 (16-ounce) jar mango or peach salsa
3 tablespoons apple cider vinegar

Purée ingredients with an immersion blender, blender, or food processor until smooth.

Store refrigerated in an airtight container for up to 1 month.

Caesar Dressing

MAKES 1 CUP; ABOUT 8 SERVINGS

I love this adaptation of the original high-fat version.

1 (16-ounce) can chickpeas/garbanzo beans
   (undrained)
¼ cup lemon juice
1 tablespoon capers (do not drain)

2 cloves garlic

1 teaspoon soy sauce

1 teaspoon black pepper

Purée all ingredients with an immersion blender, blender, or food processor until creamy.

Store refrigerated in an airtight container for up to 1 month.

Ginger-Soy Vinaigrette/ Marinade

MAKES ¾ CUP; ABOUT 6 SERVINGS

Play around with the ingredient proportions to make it your own. Splash it over salad greens or veggies and tofu before grilling.

¼ cup soy sauce

¼ cup rice wine vinegar

2 cloves garlic

2 tablespoons mirin (rice wine)

1 tablespoon fresh, chopped ginger

Purée all ingredients with an immersion blender, blender, or food processor until well chopped and blended.

Store refrigerated in an airtight container for up to 2 months.

Garlic-Balsamic Vinaigrette

MAKES 1 CUP; ABOUT 8 SERVINGS

Your house may stink for a few hours after making this, but it's totally worth it. Prepare extra to store.

1 cup balsamic vinegar
3 cloves garlic, minced
1 teaspoon fresh rosemary, chopped

In a heavy saucepan, bring all ingredients to a slow boil over medium-high heat. Simmer until vinegar is reduced by half, 10 to 20 minutes. (Or combine all ingredients in a microwave-safe bowl and cook on high in 3-minute increments until vinegar is reduced by half.)

Store refrigerated in a covered jar for up to 2 weeks.

Roasted Pepper–Balsamic Vinaigrette

MAKES 1 CUP; ABOUT 8 SERVINGS

Simple and easy. Can't mess it up.

1 large red bell pepper, cored, seeded, and halved
2 cloves garlic
½ cup balsamic vinegar

Preheat oven to 425°.

Place pepper halves on baking sheet with a clove of garlic on top of each.

Roast for 45 minutes or until skin browns, turning peppers halfway through.

Blend peppers, garlic, and vinegar in a blender or food processor until smooth. Store refrigerated in a covered jar for up to 2 weeks.

Dips, Snacks, Hors d'Oeuvres, and Kitchen Basics

The life of the party!

Roasted Red Pepper Tapenade

MAKES 2 CUPS; ABOUT 16 SERVINGS

I was actually working on a hummus recipe when I created this. It was so darn awesome that I left out the liquid and kept it as is.

1 red bell pepper, cored, seeded, and halved
2 cloves garlic
1 can chickpeas/garbanzo beans, drained
½ cup pitted olives
½ teaspoon salt

Preheat oven to 425°.

Place pepper halves on baking sheet with a clove of garlic on top of each.

Roast for 35 minutes, turning peppers halfway through.

Blend all ingredients with an immersion blender, blender, or food processor until well chopped. Serve as a dip or as a spread on a whole-wheat baguette.

Baba Ganoush (Eggplant Dip)

MAKES 1½ CUPS; ABOUT 12 SERVINGS

Great as a party dip. Make extra to use in a sandwich wrap the next day.

1 medium eggplant, peeled and sliced

2 cloves garlic

1 (15-ounce) can chickpeas/garbanzo beans, undrained

¾ teaspoon salt

¼ teaspoon cumin (optional)

1 tablespoon fresh lemon juice

Preheat oven to 425°.

Place eggplant and garlic on aluminum foil in oven and cook until soft, about 25 minutes.

Purée all ingredients, including roasted eggplant and garlic, with an immersion blender, blender, or food processor until thick and smooth.

Enjoy immediately or store in refrigerator for a few days.

White Bean Paté

MAKES 1¼ CUPS; ABOUT 10 SERVINGS

I created this by accident one day in my kitchen when I had leftover beans—and I've been making it ever since. I prefer this mild dip to classic hummus, and it sounds so much more elegant.

1 (15-ounce) can Great Northern or cannellini
    beans, drained but not rinsed
2 cloves garlic
½ teaspoon dried thyme
½ teaspoon dried rosemary
Salt, to taste

Purée all ingredients with an immersion blender, blender, or food processor until thick and smooth.

Enjoy immediately or store in refrigerator for a few days.

Hot Artichoke Dip
SERVES 12 TO 15

I just had to try to create a substitute for this party fa-vorite. My no-fat version is outrageously delicious—and you'll never miss the cheese and mayo. Promise.

1 (15-ounce) can chickpeas/garbanzo beans,
    undrained
1 (14-ounce) can artichokes, drained
2 cloves garlic
1 teaspoon salt
½ teaspoon hot sauce of choice

Preheat oven to 425°.

Purée all ingredients in a food processor or blender until thick and smooth.

Place in an oven-safe casserole and bake for 12 to 15 minutes.

Serve with whole-wheat pita or as a dip with vege-tables.

Hot Spinach Dip

SERVES 10 TO 12

Bring this to a party but don't bother telling the guests it's vegan. They won't believe you anyway.

1 pound baby spinach, steamed to wilt and
     squeezed to remove excess water
1 (15-ounce) can cannellini beans, undrained
1¼ teaspoons salt
¼ teaspoon nutmeg

Preheat oven to 425°.

Blend all ingredients with an immersion blender, blender, or food processor until smooth.

Place in an oven-safe casserole and bake for 12 to 15 minutes. Serve with whole-grain flatbread or crackers.

Cheesy Popcorn

MAKES ABOUT 10 CUPS/SERVES 3 TO 4

A great recipe adapted from my dear friend Pete's version. He used to make it in college and douse it in butter—the ultimate study-break snack. But who needs that butter now?

½ cup popcorn kernels
1 tablespoon tamari or soy sauce, or to taste
½ cup nutritional yeast
1 large brown paper grocery bag

In a small bowl, mix corn kernels with tamari.

Place corn kernels in a brown paper bag and fold bag over twice. Cook in microwave until corn popping slows down, around 3 to 4 minutes; keep watch that the bag does not catch on fire. Open carefully.

Add nutritional yeast to bag and shake well. Eat out of bag. Shake periodically to recoat popcorn, if desired.

Kettle Corn

MAKES ABOUT 10 CUPS/SERVES 3 TO 4

The perfect marriage of sweet and savory. Cue up the movie, bring out the popcorn bowls, and dig in to this simple, healthy, and tasty snack!

½ cup popcorn kernels
2½ tablespoons agave nectar or pure maple syrup,
    or 4 tablespoons sugar
2 teaspoons salt
1 large brown paper grocery bag

In a small bowl, mix corn kernels with agave nectar and salt.

Place corn kernels in a brown paper bag and fold bag over twice. Cook in microwave until corn popping slows down, around 3 to 4 minutes; keep watch that the bag does not catch on fire. Open carefully.

Eat out of bag or transfer to bowl.

Crunchy Chickpeas

MAKES 1½ CUPS/SERVES 8

Perfect for a party snack—or throw on the countertop in a bowl for the kids' munchies.

1 (15-ounce) can chickpeas/garbanzo beans,
    drained and rinsed
¼ teaspoon salt, or to taste
¼ teaspoon spice of choice (chili powder, garlic
    powder, or curry powder)

Preheat oven to 450°.

Use a paper towel to pat dry the chickpeas. Toss with salt and spice.

Bake on a foiled cookie sheet (or nonstick pan) for 30 to 40 minutes until golden brown and crunchy. Watch carefully to avoid burning. Enjoy warm or cool.

Seven-Layer Dip

SERVES 4 TO 6

Bring along as a great party dish or enjoy for a fun family meal with Baked Tortilla Chips (recipe on page 155).

1 (15-ounce) can refried beans (no added oil)
1 ripe avocado, mashed with ½ teaspoon salt
1 cup salsa fresca
1 cup sliced black olives
½ cup green chili sauce

1 cup shredded lettuce
¼ cup chopped green onion

In a 9 x 13-inch casserole pan, layer dip as follows:
—Beans
—Mashed avocado
—Salsa
—Olives
—Chili sauce
—Lettuce
—Green onions
Serve with Baked Tortilla Chips (recipe below) or fresh vegetables for dipping.

Baked Tortilla Chips

MAKES 48 CHIPS; SERVES 4

Please make extra if you want to avoid drama in the house.

12 small corn tortillas
2 tablespoons fresh lime juice
Salt, to taste

Preheat oven to 375°.

Brush tortillas on each side with lime juice. Stack tortillas and cut like a pizza into 4 wedges.

Arrange in a single layer on a baking sheet and bake for 18 minutes, turning over after 9 minutes. Watch carefully to avoid burning. Cool to harden. Toss with salt. Enjoy alone or with dip of choice.

Caprese Skewers

SERVES 8

A perfect elegant appetizer.

1 (14-ounce) box firm tofu, drained, halved, and
    cubed (make 24 cubes)
24 sun-dried tomato halves (dried, not in oil; if
    brittle, soak in warm water for 15 minutes) or
    2 large fresh tomatoes, cut into 24 chunks
24 fresh basil leaves
¼ cup balsamic glaze (or aged balsamic vinegar)
8 skewers

Skewer tofu, tomato, and basil, then repeat twice on
each skewer.

Lay all skewers on platter and drizzle with the balsamic.

Tofu Spinach Ricotta

MAKES 2 CUPS

*Perfect mixed with pasta or added to pizza. A go-to
mix; I don't know where I'd be without this creation.
Make extra and freeze.*

1 pound fresh baby spinach, steamed to wilt and
    squeezed to remove excess water (or
    frozen spinach, defrosted and squeezed)
1 (14-ounce) package silken light tofu, drained
1 teaspoon salt
¼ teaspoon nutmeg

With an immersion blender, blender, or food processor, combine all ingredients until creamy.

Use immediately or freeze and use when needed.

Breakfast, Breads, and Muffins

These will fool your taste buds and satisfy your cravings.

Whole-Wheat Blueberry Pancakes

SERVES 4

You and your family will never know the difference between these and their non-vegan rivals. My fabulous, wonderful, even-tempered (ha!) teenager, Cai, eats these with a smile. (That's right, a smile!)

1¼ cups white whole-wheat flour
   (or whole-wheat pastry flour)
2 teaspoons baking powder
¾ teaspoon salt
1⅓ cups almond milk
1 cup blueberries
1 tablespoon agave nectar or pure maple
   syrup
1 tablespoon ground flaxseed or flaxseed meal
   mixed with 3 tablespoons warm water;
   let sit 10 minutes

In a medium bowl, blend flour, baking powder, and salt.

Add remaining ingredients and mix until combined.

On a nonstick pan or griddle, pour 2 to 3 tablespoons of batter per pancake, and cook over medium-low heat. Flip when pancakes start to bubble or appear firm on edges, and cook 1 to 2 more minutes or until golden brown. Serve immediately.

Pumpkin-Pudding Pancakes
SERVES 8

These are so out-of-this-world delicious, it's worth planning a holiday brunch around them just so you can show them off.

2 cups white whole-wheat flour or
   whole-wheat pastry flour
2 teaspoons baking powder
1 teaspoon salt
2 teaspoons ground cinnamon
½ teaspoon nutmeg
½ cup chopped walnuts (optional)
2 tablespoons agave nectar or pure maple syrup
2 cups almond milk
1 tablespoon ground flaxseed or flaxseed meal
   mixed with 3 tablespoons warm water; let sit 10
   minutes
1 cup canned pumpkin (not pumpkin pie filling)

Mix flour, baking powder, salt, cinnamon, nutmeg, and nuts (optional).

In a separate bowl, combine remaining ingredients and mix well. Add to flour mixture and mix until well combined.

On a nonstick pan or griddle, pour 2 to 3 tablespoons of batter per pancake, and cook over low heat. Flip when pancakes start to bubble or appear firm on edges, and cook 1 to 2 more minutes. Center may remain moist like pudding. Serve immediately.

Breakfast Burritos

SERVES 4

No one makes scrambled eggs and bacon like my dad. Once you throw these great ingredients together and wrap them up in a tortilla, however, it rivals his breakfasts—without the increased risk of cardiac arrest.

½ cup chopped onion

2 cloves garlic, minced

½ cup red or green bell peppers, cored, seeded, and chopped

1 (14-ounce) box firm tofu, drained, chopped, and crumbled into small pieces

1 cup salsa, divided

½ teaspoon turmeric

½ teaspoon salt

4 whole-wheat tortillas (burrito size)

In a heavy dry pan, sauté onions over medium heat until light brown. Add garlic and peppers and cook 2 more minutes. If ingredients begin to stick, add water, ¼ cup at a time.

Add tofu, ¼ cup of salsa, turmeric, and salt and cook until heated.

Divide mixture in four, roll inside tortilla, and top with remaining salsa.

Granola

MAKES EIGHT ½-CUP SERVINGS

I formally apologize to my husband for all the terrible soggy granolas I cobbled together prior to this winner. Thanks to my loyal kitchen assistant, Meg, we finally figured it out.

3 cups quick-cooking oats
¼ cup sunflower seeds, unsalted
¼ cup chopped nuts of choice (optional)
1 cup raisins
½ teaspoon salt
6 tablespoons water
2 tablespoons agave nectar or pure maple syrup
1 teaspoon vanilla extract

Preheat oven to 250°.

In a medium bowl, mix together oats, seeds, nuts, and raisins.

In a separate small bowl, whisk together salt, water, agave nectar, and vanilla. Add to oat mixture, tossing or using hands to coat evenly.

Spread mixture in a single layer on a large cookie sheet. Bake for 60 minutes, tossing every 20 minutes. Cool and serve. Store in an airtight container.

Banana Overnight Oatmeal

SERVES 2

I fondly remember inviting my coworker at People magazine (and now coauthor) Lisa over for Valentine's Day brunch in New York City—and trying to impress her with my delicious, much-bragged-about Irish oatmeal. Too bad she had to wait more than an hour and a half before it was ready to eat. Who knew that steel-cut oats took so long to cook? Well, my dear friend, Valentine, and collaborator, now I know the trick.

4 cups water
1 cup steel-cut Irish oats
2 ripe bananas, cut into small chunks

In a small heavy saucepan, bring water to a boil.
Add oats and bananas, stir, and cover.
Remove pot from heat and *do not uncover* until morning. Reheat when ready to eat.

Apple-Cinnamon Muesli

SERVES 2 TO 4

When my wonderful friend Jamie came back from a dance conference raving about the chef and her delicious breakfast muesli, I flew into a (quiet) jealous rage and concocted this version. Phew. My status as Jamie's favorite chef was once again secure.

2 cups apple juice

1 cup rolled oats

¼ cup raisins

¼ cup chopped nuts (almonds, walnuts, pecans, coconut, or other personal fave)

½ teaspoon ground cinnamon

Combine all ingredients in a bowl and cover. Soak overnight in refrigerator.

Drain extra liquid, if desired. Store in sealed container in refrigerator. Serve chilled or at room temperature or heat in microwave.

Perfect Cereal Bowl

SERVES 1

My husband makes this crunchy combo every single morning. I think he could just pre-mix the ingredients (minus the berries and almond milk); however, I do not want to squelch his desire to "cook."

¼ cup rolled oats (uncooked)

¼ cup oil-free granola or Ezekiel Cereal

¼ cup Nature's Path Smart Bran

1 tablespoon ground flaxseed or flaxseed meal

½ cup berries

Almond milk (or other nondairy milk of choice)

Combine all ingredients except milk in a cereal bowl. Add nondairy milk of choice and enjoy.

Breakfast Parfait

SERVES 2

This is a great way to trick yourself into thinking you're eating a big, sinful treat. Makes a great snack, too!

2 cups vanilla soy, almond, or coconut
    yogurt
1 cup mixed berries
¾ cup oil-free granola or Ezekiel Cinnamon Raisin
    Cereal

Layer yogurt, fruit, granola in a tall glass, and repeat layer. Enjoy!

Power Breakfast/Snack Bars

SERVES 10 TO 12

I created these bars as a perfect light meal to nosh on the go or as a pre- or post-workout snack. Make a ton and wrap and freeze in individual squares, since they are so much better than any store-bought version.

1¼ cups rolled oats
1 cup shredded coconut
¾ cup sunflower seeds, unsalted
1 cup raisins, dried cranberries, dark chocolate
    chips (vegan), or combo
⅓ cup ground flaxseed or flaxseed meal
1 cup almond butter

½ teaspoon salt
¾ teaspoon ground cinnamon
1 cup warm water

Preheat oven to 350°.

Mix all ingredients in a bowl (using your hands will help). Add more water, a tablespoon at a time, if necessary to get ingredients to stick together.

Firmly press mixture into a 9 x 13-inch baking dish.

Bake for 30 minutes. Cool completely (2 to 3 hours) before slicing into small squares.

Corn Bread

SERVES 6 TO 8

I thought this could not be better until my friend and kitchen assistant of the day, Miriam, stated in her adorable Southern accent, "Where I come from, we just add a bit of bacon grease to the pan to flavor it up." Oh well, I tried.

1 cup white whole-wheat flour or whole-wheat
   pastry flour
1 cup cornmeal
4 teaspoons baking powder
¾ teaspoon salt
⅓ cup agave nectar or pure maple syrup
2 tablespoons ground flaxseed or flaxseed meal
   soaked in 6 tablespoons warm water; let sit for
   10 minutes

1 cup unsweetened plain almond milk

¼ cup applesauce

1 cup canned corn, drained

Preheat oven to 350°.

In a medium bowl, whisk together flour, cornmeal, baking powder, and salt until well combined.

In a separate bowl, mix agave nectar, flaxseed mixture, almond milk, applesauce, and corn. Add to the flour mixture and mix until well blended.

Pour into nonstick baking pan or muffin tins. Bake for 30 to 40 minutes, or until bread is firm to touch. Cool and serve.

Blueberry-Banana Muffins

MAKES 18 MUFFINS

This is one of my earlier vegan recipes. I would only inform a few clients when I was baking these, because I could not keep up with the demand.

1¾ cups white whole-wheat flour or whole-wheat pastry flour

2¼ teaspoons baking powder

½ teaspoon salt

1 cup fresh or frozen blueberries

3 ripe bananas, mashed

½ cup agave nectar or pure maple syrup

⅓ cup applesauce

2 tablespoons ground flaxseed or flaxseed meal
    mixed with 6 tablespoons warm water; let sit
    for 10 minutes

Preheat oven to 350°.

In a medium bowl, mix flour, baking powder, and salt.

In a separate medium bowl, mix remaining ingredients. Add to flour mixture and combine until blended.

Pour in a nonstick muffin pan (or line muffin pan with paper-cup liners) and bake for 30 minutes. Cool and serve.

Power Muffins

MAKES 18 MUFFINS

A great grab-and-go snack that can even power up my Energizer-bunny sister-in-law before a day of hiking, yoga, and climbing up mountains then skiing down. Want to keep up with her? Eat these muffins, which are chock-full of energy-boosting ingredients.

1 tablespoon chia seeds

2 tablespoons wheat germ

1½ cups white whole-wheat flour or whole-wheat
    pastry flour

2 teaspoons baking soda

½ teaspoon salt

½ teaspoon ground cinnamon

¼ teaspoon nutmeg

1 cup canned pumpkin (not pumpkin pie filling)

½ cup applesauce

½ cup pure maple syrup

½ cup almond milk

½ cup raisins

2 tablespoons ground flaxseed or flaxseed meal
    mixed with 6 tablespoons warm water; let sit
    for 10 minutes

Preheat oven to 350°.

In a large bowl, toss together chia seeds, wheat germ, flour, baking soda, salt, cinnamon, and nutmeg.

In a separate bowl, mix remaining ingredients and add to flour mixture. Mix until well blended.

Pour in nonstick muffin pan (or line muffin pan with paper cup liners) and bake for 30 minutes. Cool and serve.

Nut Butter

MAKES 1¼ CUPS; 8 TO 10 SERVINGS

Making your own nut butter is so easy. You won't believe it works until you try it yourself!

2 cups almonds, cashews, or peanuts

Place nuts in a food processor and blend on high.

If nuts get stuck to sides or bottom of food processor, scrape down and continue blending until desired consistency is reached, about 10 minutes for creamy. (Trust me, it will become smooth and awesome.)

Store refrigerated in a sealed container for up to a month.

Desserts and Sweet Treats

Frozen Banana Butter Treats

MAKES 12 TO 14 TREATS

My soccer-goalie daughter, Liv, adores these. They're a great snack after soccer games, where she spends afternoons diving headfirst for balls while large girls with pointy cleats come this close to kicking her face in (sorry for the graphic commentary).

2 bananas, sliced into ½-inch-thick coins

½ cup almond butter, peanut butter, or apple butter

Spread about ½ teaspoon of nut or apple butter on half of the banana coins. Top with remaining coins to make individual sandwiches.

Place all sandwiches on a plate, pan, or tinfoil, and cover. Freeze until hardened.

Chocolate-Banana Dessert Shake

MAKES 2 SERVINGS

I think my son, Cam, created this recipe. Since I don't remember, I will attribute it to him anyway so I can remain his "favorite mom ever"!

2 bananas, peeled (frozen for a thicker shake)
1 cup almond milk
3–4 ice cubes
¼ teaspoon unsweetened cocoa powder

Combine all ingredients in a blender until smooth. Pour into glasses and enjoy!

Baked Apple
SERVES 4

My mom taught me to make baked apples as a child. Back then, I think she doused them with diet soda to make them "healthier." Wow, how times have changed!

2 tablespoons pure maple syrup
2 tablespoons raisins
½ teaspoon ground cinnamon
4 large apples, cores removed but not
    cut through bottom

Preheat oven to 350°.

Toss together maple syrup, raisins, and cinnamon.

Divide mixture into 4 parts and place in well of each apple.

Place stuffed apples on a baking sheet, cover with foil, and bake for 40 minutes (or longer for softer baked apple). Enjoy while still warm or chill to serve.

Poached Pears

SERVES 4 TO 8

The perfect finish to an elegant dinner.

1 cup red or port wine
¼ cup agave nectar or pure maple syrup
½ cup water
½ teaspoon ground cinnamon
4 ripe pears, peeled, cored, and halved

In a pan large enough to lay pear halves flat, simmer wine, agave nectar, water, and cinnamon for 5 minutes.

Add pears facedown, cover, and simmer an additional 10 minutes, turning pears over after 5 minutes.

Serve warm or chilled (store in liquid for stronger flavor).

OPTIONAL: Top with dried cranberries and/or oil-free granola.

Apple Cobbler

SERVES 4

To try it is to love it. I have been making this healthy version forever. It is great fresh out of the oven or as a leftover the next day. (Although, I wouldn't really know, since someone always finishes it off before I can get there.)

6 cups chopped apples, peeled or unpeeled

¼ cup plus 2 tablespoons white whole-wheat flour
   or whole-wheat pastry flour, divided

¼ cup brown sugar, divided

1 teaspoon ground cinnamon, divided

¼ teaspoon salt

¼ cup rolled oats

1 tablespoon almond milk

Preheat oven to 350°.

Toss apples with 2 tablespoons of the flour, 2 tablespoons of the brown sugar, and ½ teaspoon of the cinnamon. Place in an 8- or 9-inch round casserole dish.

With a fork, blend/toss remaining ingredients until the consistency is crumbly. Spoon over apple mixture.

Bake covered for 35 to 45 minutes until apples are tender. Serve warm.

Chocolate Chip Biscotti
SERVES 8 TO 12

Since going vegan, I've been attempting to make an awesome vegan cookie to appease my sweet tooth. I love biscotti and have finally created a version that I am proud to call my own. They're as yummy as the unhealthy delights my oldest, dearest friend Jill and I used to make when we were kids.

1¾ cups white whole-wheat flour or whole-wheat
   pastry flour

¼ teaspoon salt

1 teaspoon baking powder

¾ cup walnuts, chopped

⅔ cup dark chocolate chips (vegan)

½ cup agave nectar or pure maple syrup

1 teaspoon vanilla extract

2 tablespoons ground flaxseed or flaxseed meal
    combined with 6 tablespoons hot water; let sit
    10 minutes

Preheat oven to 350°.

In a medium bowl, combine flour, salt, baking powder, nuts, and chocolate and mix well.

In a separate bowl, combine agave nectar, vanilla, and flaxseed mixture. Add to flour mixture and combine, using hands to mix if necessary.

With flour-dusted hands, divide the dough into 2 parts and roll each into 3-inch-wide logs, around ¾-inch high.

Bake on a tinfoil-lined cookie sheet for 30 minutes. Remove pan and let sit for 20 minutes. Reduce oven temperature to 325°.

Slice logs into ½-inch slices, lay on side, and return to oven for 24 minutes, flipping cookies after 12 minutes. Cool to harden.

Chocolate Birthday Cake

SERVES 10 TO 12

Yes, vegans can have their cake . . . and eat it, too! When my amazing friend Meg surprised me with this deli-

cious birthday cake, I thought I had died and gone to heaven. And because it's for a special occasion, we indulged in white flour and sugar.

1½ cups flour
¾ cup sugar
¼ cup cocoa powder
1 teaspoon baking soda
½ teaspoon salt
1 cup water
½ cup applesauce
2 teaspoons vanilla extract
2 teaspoons balsamic vinegar
¼ cup powdered sugar

Preheat oven to 350°.

Line a 9-inch round cake pan with wax paper.

In a mixing bowl, sift together flour, sugar, cocoa powder, baking soda, and salt. Add water, applesauce, vanilla, and vinegar and mix thoroughly.

Pour into cake pan and bake 30 to 35 minutes. Cool well and sprinkle with powdered sugar. Add birthday candles and serve.

To make a layer cake, double the recipe and bake two cakes. When cool, place strawberries between layers.

Chocolate Mousse

SERVES 6

Okay, I admit it. I am a chocoholic, but it's not my fault. I come from a long line of so-called chocoholics. I think even my dear sister, a self-professed master chocoholic, would love this. When you must be naughty, you'll enjoy it, too.

1 (12-ounce) package firm silken light tofu, drained
1¼ cups dark chocolate chips (vegan)
2 tablespoons agave nectar or pure maple syrup

Using a food processor, blender, or hand mixer, blend tofu until just smooth.

In a double boiler, melt chocolate chips over low heat, stirring constantly.

Blend chocolate, agave nectar, and tofu with a blender or immersion blender until smooth. Spoon into 6 small cups. Chill and serve. (For a quick chill, place cups in freezer for 15 minutes.)

Pumpkin Mousse

SERVES 8

Such a wonderful fall treat.

1 (15-ounce) can pumpkin (not pumpkin pie filling)
1 (12-ounce) package firm silken light tofu, drained
4 tablespoons pure maple syrup
1 teaspoon vanilla extract

¾ teaspoon to 1 teaspoon ground cinnamon
¼ teaspoon to ½ teaspoon nutmeg
¼ teaspoon salt
Pinch allspice (optional)

Using a food processor, blender, or hand mixer, blend all ingredients until smooth.

Spoon into 8 small cups. Chill and serve. (For a quick chill, place cups in freezer for 15 minutes.)

Mango Sorbet
SERVES 4

When I created this, I literally licked the leftovers out of my food processor.

1 pound (2 cups) frozen mango chunks (take out
   of freezer 5 minutes before making)
2 tablespoons powdered sugar or 1 teaspoon
   agave nectar or pure maple syrup
1 tablespoon canned light coconut milk;
   shake can before opening (for a lower-fat option, substitute 1 tablespoon plain almond milk
   mixed with a dash of coconut extract)

Place all ingredients in a food processor. Blend well until smooth, about 1½ to 2 minutes.

Eat immediately or freeze in a sealed container for a firmer sorbet.

Peach Pie Smoothie Bowl
SERVES 3 TO 4

My friend and advisor is the creator of Rush Bowls—a sort of frozen smoothie that's blended with other delights and served in a bowl. I'm addicted to them and came up with this recipe so I could eat my own version of the bowls at a whim. Whip this up—and then head to the freezer section of your grocery store to try other Rush Bowl flavors.

¾ cup almond milk

½ cup peach or apple juice

1 pound (2 cups) frozen peach slices

1 banana, peeled and frozen

1 teaspoon agave nectar or pure maple syrup

1 teaspoon ground cinnamon

1 teaspoon vanilla

½ cup granola or other cereal of choice

Place all ingredients, except granola, in a blender. Mix until creamy.

To serve, top with oil-free granola or cereal.

Banana-Chocolate Mousse
SERVES 4

Who doesn't love mousse? This version is simple, light, and easy.

4 sliced bananas (2 cups), frozen
2 tablespoons powdered sugar or 1 teaspoon
    agave nectar
1 tablespoon canned light coconut milk; shake can
    before opening (for a lower-fat option, substi-
    tute 1 tablespoon plain almond milk mixed with
    a dash of coconut extract)
¼ cup unsweetened cocoa powder

Place all ingredients in a food processor. Blend well until smooth, about 1½ to 2 minutes.

Eat immediately or chill for firmer mousse.

Chia Pudding
SERVES 4 TO 6

Wow! If you like tapioca or rice pudding, you'll adore this super-healthy treat.

2½ cups almond milk
3 tablespoons agave nectar or pure maple syrup
½ cup chia seeds
½ teaspoon vanilla extract (eliminate if using
    maple syrup)

¼ teaspoon nutmeg
½ teaspoon ground cinnamon

Stir all ingredients together in a jar or airtight container.

Cover tightly and refrigerate for 4 hours (shake or stir vigorously after 2 hours).

Stir well before serving.

Now Let's Party!

Celebrate Your Vegan Transformation with a Party—Or a Year's Worth!

Now that you're a vegan, it's time to celebrate—and show your friends and family how easy, fun, and delicious it is. Don't know what to make? We've done the planning for you. All you need to do is show up (and do a little prep work).

Most of these dishes can be prepared in advance, so you don't have to go crazy at the last minute—nor do you have to fret about the mayonnaise spoiling, the meat rotting, or the cheese going rancid. And, don't forget, alcohol is vegan, so whip out the blender and bring on the cocktails!

The monotony of making the old standards is gone. Here is a whole year's worth of vegan parties.

Asian Fusion

I keep most of these ingredients in my house at all times. When in a big rush (which is the norm for me), I choose to make just one or two of these recipes. Each is truly satisfying.

- White Miso Noodle Soup (recipe on page 136)
- Vegetable Fried Rice (recipe on page 97)
- Pad Thai (recipe on page 106)
- Spicy Thai String Beans and Tofu (recipe on page 112)

Brunch

For years, I've been making vegan blueberry pancakes for my family and friends, and no one—I mean no one—ever realized that these tasty treats were free of fat, dairy, and eggs. I remember serving them at a brunch once, while my friend made the standard non-vegan version. Mine were gobbled up immediately and his were simply getting cold on the counter.

- Whole-Wheat Blueberry Pancakes (recipe on page 157)
- Pumpkin-Pudding Pancakes (recipe on page 158)
- Breakfast Burritos (recipe on page 159)
- Chilaquiles (recipe on page 107)

Comfort Food

Oh, baby, it's cold outside. Whip up this heart- and soul-warming menu, grab a blanket, and camp out in front of the fireplace.

- Creamy Corn Chowder (recipe on page 134)
- Shepherd's Pie (recipe on page 102)
- Oven-Roasted Root Vegetables (recipe on page 123)
- Baked Apple (recipe on page 169)

French Gourmet

Oui, oui, vegan meals can definitely be romantic, elegant, and chic!

- White Bean Paté (recipe on page 150)
- Cassoulet (recipe on page 111)
- Mushroom Risotto (recipe on page 95)
- Ratatouille (recipe on page 129)
- Chocolate Mousse (recipe on page 174)

Italian Feast

My family's favorite dishes. I make a combination of these when I'm trying to win over the little darlings ("Clean your rooms, and Mom will make you an Italian feast, kids.").

- Pasta e Fagioli (recipe on page 138)
- Caesar Feast (recipe on page 144)
- Italian Vegetable Terrine (recipe on page 108)

- Baked Ziti/Spaghetti Pie (recipe on page 109)
- Eggplant "Parmesan" (recipe on page 94)
- Chocolate Chip Biscotti (recipe on page 171)

Kid-Friendly

When I first started exploring vegan cooking, my kids would ask, "Why is everything brown and mushy?" Not exactly what I wanted to hear after spending hours in the kitchen trying to improve their health (ungrateful little munchkins). Thus, I've spent many more hours in the kitchen trying to invent nutritious and delicious dishes my kids would love. (Now who's your favorite mama?)

- Cheesy Popcorn (recipe on page 152)
- Macaroni and Cheese (recipe on page 103)
- Tomato-Basil Bisque (recipe on page 135)
- Frozen Banana Butter Treats (recipe on page 168)

Latin Fiesta

Sangria and margaritas are vegan. ¡Olé!

- Seven-Layer Dip (recipe on page 154)
- Chiles Rellenos (recipe on page 96)
- Southwest Black-Bean Soup (recipe on page 133)
- Paella (recipe on page 117)
- Mango Sorbet (recipe on page 175)

Mother's Day/Shower Luncheon

I love girlie parties! How fun to spend an afternoon relaxing, chatting with friends, and eating healthy vegan treats.

- Thai Peanut Noodles (recipe on page 121)
- Asian Salad (recipe on page 144), topped with Ginger-Soy Vinaigrette (recipe on page 147)
- Chocolate Mousse—make in shot glasses (recipe on page 174)
- Pumpkin Mousse—make in shot glasses (recipe on page 174)
- Banana-Chocolate Mousse—make in shot glasses (recipe on page 177)

Passage to India

Hands down, Indian is my favorite cuisine. Since most Indian restaurants use ghee (clarified butter) and other fats and oils in their dishes, it's extremely challenging to eat a healthy Indian feast without the post-meal bellyache. This menu will solve that problem.

- Curried Butternut Squash Soup (recipe on page 132)
- Chana Masala (recipe on page 105)
- Saag Paneer (recipe on page 104)
- Brown rice
- Whole-wheat pita bread
- Chia Pudding (recipe on page 177)

Picnic

Vegan picnics are awesome. They're so easy to prepare for, plus you don't have to worry about the mayo spoiling!

- Potato–Black Bean Salad (recipe on page 122)
- Caprese Skewers (recipe on page 156)
- Creamy Gazpacho (recipe on page 139)
- Mujaddara (Lebanese Lentils; recipe on page 116)
- Puttanesca Fresca (recipe on page 127)

Pizza Party

This is a fun treat for the family. Keep the party small or make some pizzas in advance and invite the whole neighborhood!

- Caesar Feast (recipe on page 144) topped with Caesar dressing (recipe on page 146)
- Veggie Pizza (recipe on page 114)
- BBQ Tofu Pizza (recipe on page 115)
- Mango Sorbet (recipe on page 175)

Super Bowl/ World Series/Sporting Event

The boys are coming over and they can eat! No need to worry. This simple menu will satisfy them while keeping you out of the kitchen to enjoy the game (or the cool commercials).

- Hot Artichoke Dip (recipe on page 151)
- Hot Spinach Dip (recipe on page 152)
- Kettle Corn (recipe on page 153)
- Crunchy Chickpeas (recipe on page 154)
- Three-Bean Chili with Smoked Tempeh (recipe on page 117)
- Corn Bread (recipe on page 164)

Thanksgiving/Holidays

I can hear my wonderful mom's New York–accented voice as I write this: "Amy, you must serve your guests turkey on Thanksgiving!" Well, guess what, Mom? Every year, my Thanksgiving table grows. Invite them and they will come. Not only that, but my tryptophan-free guests feel much more energetic after the meal, which means I have more helpers in the kitchen for cleanup duty.

- Pumpkin-Quinoa Soup (recipe on page 141)
- Brazilian Vegetable Stew (recipe on page 99)
- Oven-Roasted Root Vegetables (recipe on page 123)
- Stuffed Cabbage (recipe on page 119)
- Perfect Mashed Potatoes (recipe on page 125)
- Apple Cobbler (recipe on page 170)
- Pumpkin Mouse (recipe on page 174)

16

On the Road

Every vegan knows that eating away from home can be a challenge, but with a little preparation, traveling—even with kids—can be a piece of cake. Here are some yummy snacks to pack when hitting the road.

Keep in the Car:
- Dry-roasted or raw almonds (Amy loves tamari flavored), cashews, pecans, or walnuts
- Seeds (Amy loves pumpkin; Lisa's a sucker for sunflower)
- Vegan snack bars—stick to those with as few ingredients as possible, like Lara Bars and Clif Fruit and Nut bars
- Dried fruit—look for those with no added sugar or sulfites

- Cereal—whole grain, high fiber, all natural, no added oils
- Snack bags with your favorite combination of nuts, seeds, dried fruit, and a *few* vegan dark chocolate chips

Grab Fresh Before Leaving:
- Fruit—such as apples, cherries, grapes, and pears
- Small bag of fresh veggies
- Small bag with hummus for dipping veggies (if it will not sit in hot car too long)
- Baked Tortilla Chips (recipe on page 155) with a side of Baba Ganoush (recipe on page 150)
- Power Breakfast Bars (recipe on page 163)
- Blueberry-Banana Muffins (recipe on page 165) or Power Muffins (recipe on page 166)
- Almond, coconut, or soy yogurt (if you plan to consume in the next hour; don't forget the spoon!)

Fun Eats:
- Popcorn or popped sorghum tossed with spices like cayenne, curry, or oregano (use an air popper or place kernels in a brown bag and pop in the microwave for 3 to 4 minutes)
- Cheesy Popcorn (recipe on page 152) or Kettle Corn (recipe on page 153)
- Frozen grapes and banana slices
- Kale chips
- Crunchy Chickpeas (recipe on page 154)
- Dark chocolate squares (in moderation)

Easy-to-Pack Lunches (All Great at Room Temperature):

- Whole-wheat tortilla or Lawash flatbread (no added oils if possible), stuffed with hummus, lettuce, sliced tomatoes, and any other veggies you like (for more wrap ideas, check out the recipes on pages 143–145)
- Whole-wheat tortilla or Lawash flatbread with black beans (right out of can, drained) and fresh salsa; add sliced or mashed avocado or leftover brown rice
- Leftover whole-wheat pasta with veggies
- Whole-wheat toasted bread with almond butter and sliced banana—Amy's favorite
- The great American standby (and Lisa's personal fave): peanut-butter-and-jelly sandwich

Navigating the Social Scene

How to Handle Party Invitations from
Carnivorous Friends . . . Plus Other Practical
Tips for Avoiding Potentially Awkward
Moments on the Social Circuit

Things can get admittedly tricky when you've been invited to a friend's house for a meal or you're headed to a wedding or other event. Not only have you lost control of your food choice, but you don't want to be rude or insulting to the host by turning your nose up at her mini cocktail dogs and bacon quiche. Here are some practical tips for negotiating the social scene with grace, elegance, and finesse.

When Invited to a Friend's House

Let your host know you're vegan when you RSVP. We try to throw a little humorous self-deprecation into the mix by saying, "I'm a problem child when it comes to eating, and I don't do meat or dairy." We emphasize that we don't want them to go out of their way or make anything special (although they usually will), and we always offer to bring a vegan dish. (For some great appetizer suggestions, check out the recipes in Dips, Snacks, and Hors d'Oeuvres on page 149.)

When Invited to the Home of Someone You Don't Know

Say your date invites you to dinner at his aunt's house—and you've never met the carnivorous Aunt Elsie. If your date is comfortable bringing up the "problem child" thing to his relative, great. Otherwise, bring a vegan hostess gift and do your best to wing it—push and pick your way around what you're served. You may want to eat a hearty snack in advance just in case there are no vegan options.

When Going to a Wedding or Other Big Shindig

If appropriate, call the caterer or banquet hall before the event, explain your vegan situation, and see if they can accommodate you. Otherwise, once you're at the wedding or bat mitzvah, whisper to the server when the meal is being served and ask if he or she can bring you extra veggies, a salad, and/or a plate of pasta with marinara and vegetables.

Quick Tips for Eating Out

Let Someone Else Do the Cooking Tonight? Oh, Yeah, We're All Over That!

We love eating out and haven't shied away from the restaurant scene since switching teams. Still, navigating that world—where you're no longer in control of the kitchen—can be dicey at first.

When the menu screams, "Fettuccine Alfredo!" "Buffalo wings!" "Lobster bisque!" you may want to turn on your heels and run. But hold your horses. With a few little tricks, you'll be chowing down like a champ.

1. Communicate with the Server

If the restaurant doesn't offer any obvious vegan choices—you're at a steakhouse or rib joint, for example—let your server know the deal and ask for suggestions. Give him or her the rundown.

I Avoid:

- All meat, including beef, pork, and poultry
- Anything prepared with meat, poultry, or fish stock
- Dairy (butter, cream, cheese, milk, ice cream, yogurt, whipped cream, and so forth)
- Eggs
- Fish/shellfish

I Dig:

- Beans and legumes
- Fruits and vegetables
- Grains
- Nuts and seeds
- Olive oil (limited)
- Pasta—preferably whole wheat (provided it's not made with eggs)
- Potatoes
- Soy-based protein (tofu and tempeh)
- Wheat-based protein (seitan)

Even the most meat-centric restaurants serve greens. So if all else fails and nothing on the menu appears edible, just ask for a plate of vegetables with plain (and preferably brown) rice or simple potatoes. We've found that chefs readily accommodate these requests, sometimes fashioning gorgeous dishes of towering greens that even our carnivorous friends lust after.

2. Chat with the Chef

If something appears vegan but may not be—say, pastas made with egg, soups made with chicken broth, or veggie burgers made with cheese—ask to speak with the chef. He or she can give you the scoop and help you find vegan-friendly options.

3. Be a Good Sport

Sometimes it happens: You end up at a greasy spoon or the local burger haunt because your fraternity bros need a big, fat, greasy bacon cheeseburger. Do your best to go with the flow now and then and make do with limited choices. We try not to be whiny, angry, pain-in-the-butt vegans. (We also keep snacks with us at all times.)

We live in a country where 97 percent of the population eats meat (which includes most of our friends and family members), so we strive to be flexible—and hope our good example will win over some converts.

Restaurant Survival Guide

What's on the menu? There's something for every vegan at most restaurants. Here are the most common cuisines and the vegan menu options we recommend for each.

||||||||||||||||||||||||||||||||||||||||||||||||||||||||||||||||||||||||||||||||||||||||||||||||||||||||||||||||||||

NOTE: We know that eliminating oils when eating out can be tricky, so we encourage you to do the best you can and make your choices wisely. If you're a heart patient, avoid all dishes containing avocado, chocolate, coconut, nuts, oils, peanuts, and seeds.

||||||||||||||||||||||||||||||||||||||||||||||||||||||||||||||||||||||||||||||||||||||||||||||||||||||||||||||||||||

AMERICAN

Vegan menu options:

- Baked potato or sweet potato (no butter or sour cream)

- Rice and other grains
- Steamed vegetables
- Tossed salad with light or oil-free dressing on the side
- Veggie burgers (confirm if vegan; some are made with eggs and/or cheese)

BREAKFAST

Vegan menu options:

- Fruit
- Oatmeal (confirm that it's made without milk)
- Pancakes, if made without eggs or milk (a rarity, but worth asking)
- Veggie "egg" burrito without eggs (yup, just veggies in a burrito)—request with tofu and salsa, if available
- Veggie "omelet" without eggs—one of Lisa's faves; basically sautéed vegetables; request with tofu and salsa, if available
- Whole-wheat toast—with jam or peanut butter

CHINESE

Vegan menu options:

- Brown rice (if available)
- Oil-free sauces for dipping, such as sweet-chili sauce and low-sodium soy sauce
- Steamed vegetables with steamed tofu

DESSERT

Vegan menu options:

- Dark chocolate
- Dark chocolate–covered strawberries and fruit

- Fresh fruit
- Sorbet
- Ask about other options—for example, some cobblers can be made without animal products

GREEK
Vegan menu options:

- Baba ganoush
- Falafel (go easy, since these are typically fried)
- Greek salad (omit the feta cheese; request light dressing on the side)
- Hummus
- Stuffed grape leaves
- Tabbouleh

INDIAN
Vegan menu options:

- Any vegetarian dishes that don't contain ghee (clarified butter) or any other dairy (be sure to ask, since many menu items are prepared with these ingredients)
  - Try to avoid dishes with too much rich coconut milk; if you're craving that intensity, ask if they can go lighter in your dish
- Brown rice (if available)
- Mango chutney or spicy dipping sauces
- Vegan breads (ask); eat in limited quantities, since they often contain oil

ITALIAN

Vegan menu options:

- Marinara or pomodoro sauce (check if it has any cheese or meat in it)
- Pasta (whole wheat, if possible) with marinara (check if vegan and low oil)
  - Add:
    Chopped tomatoes
    Fresh broccoli
    Mushrooms
    Onions
    Peppers
    Spinach
    White beans
- Tossed salad (no cheese or meat) with balsamic vinegar

JAPANESE/SUSHI

Vegan menu options:

- Bowl of buckwheat udon soup (if soup is vegetable based)
- Brown rice (if available)
- Steamed tofu
- Vegetable dishes (steamed, if possible, with vegan sauce—like soy or dumpling—on the side)
- Vegetable, sweet potato, or futomaki roll without egg or fish

MEXICAN

Vegan menu options:

- Black, pinto, or refried beans (ask if vegan and check for fat; refried beans are often mashed pinto beans with seasoning)
- Grilled vegetables (request no/little oil)
- Guacamole (ask if vegan; enjoy in limited quantities)
- Plain corn tortillas (not fried)
- Rice (ask if vegan and low oil/no lard)
- Salsa fresca/pico de gallo

PIZZERIA

Vegan menu options:

- Pizza (whole wheat if possible; omit cheese)
- Tomato sauce (ask if has any cheese in it)
- Tossed salad (no cheese or meat) with balsamic vinegar or low-fat dressing
- Vegetable toppings

THAI

Vegan menu options:

- Brown rice (if available)
- Oil-free sauces for dipping, such as sweet-chili sauce and low-sodium soy sauce
- Rice noodles with vegetables
  - Ask for no oil and vegan sauce on the side (many traditional sauces contain fish, so be specific)
- Steamed vegetables with steamed tofu

Surviving the
Restaurant Chains

There's one on every corner, so we might as well learn to live harmoniously with the chain restaurants—which is a lot easier than you may think. Many of these eateries—even the unlikeliest (Denny's? Cheesecake Factory?)—offer a surprising variety of options for vegan palates.

We scoured the menus of the top chains and compiled a list of vegan-friendly choices. Just know that menu items were accurate at press time and may have changed since publication. Also, choices may differ between franchises. We've provided each restaurant's website address so you can check menus and nutritional information before you go.

One simple rule: learn to be creative about veganizing dishes by deleting the verboten ingredients and adding in the good stuff. Most restaurants are happy to accommodate you.

ONE BEGRUDGING NOTE: Okay, we know it's not much fun to munch on vegetables while your BFF's are inhaling Big Macs. So if it's killing you to watch your compadres knock back 1,140-calorie Triple Whoppers, go ahead and order some french fries or onion rings (small, not jumbo size!). But please do this only once in a blue moon, as they are full of calories, fat, and sodium. (Guilty as charged: We indulge now and then.)

CAVEAT FOR HEART PATIENTS: Avoid all menu options containing avocado, coconut, nuts, seeds, chocolate, and fats. Everyone else, consume these in moderation.

APPLEBEE'S—NATIONAL CHAIN
applebees.com

- Applesauce
- Baked potato (hold the butter and sour cream)
- Black bean corn salsa
- Crispy red potatoes
- Fiesta Chicken Chopped Salad (hold the chicken)
- Fruit
- Guacamole
- Penne or fettuccine with marinara (request)
- Seasonal Berry & Spinach Salad (skip the chicken and cheese) with fat-free Italian dressing
- Steamed vegetables

ARBY'S—NATIONAL CHAIN
arbys.com

- Apple
- Apple and cherry turnover (only if you must)
- Chopped Farmhouse Salad (nix the chicken, pepper bacon, and cheese) with light Italian dressing
- Chopped side salad (hold the cheese) with light Italian dressing
- French fries (only if desperate)

ATLANTA BREAD—LOCATIONS IN 20 STATES
atlantabread.com

- Bagels: wheat, whole grain
- Balsamic Bleu Salad (nix the cheese)
- Breads: sourdough, nine grain, whole grain, honey wheat, rye, and pumpernickel
- California Avocado Sandwich (no cheese or dill sauce)
- Fruit salad
- Garden vegetable soup
- Greek salad (nix the cheese) with fat-free raspberry vinaigrette
- House salad with fat-free raspberry vinaigrette
- Italian Vegetarian Panini (no cheese)
- Veggie sandwich (nix the cheese and the dill sauce)

AU BON PAIN—LOCATIONS IN 23 STATES AND DISTRICT OF COLUMBIA
aubonpain.com

- 12 veggies soup
- Artisan honey multigrain baguette
- Barley and creamy lentil soup
- Black bean soup
- Broccoli and carrots
- Carrot ginger soup
- Curried rice and lentil soup
- French Moroccan tomato lentil soup
- Fresh fruit
- Gazpacho
- Green beans
- Oatmeal
- Side garden salad with light olive oil vinaigrette or fat-free raspberry vinaigrette
- Vegetarian Deluxe Salad (minus the cheese)
- Whole wheat multigrain bread
- Whole wheat skinny bagel

BAJA FRESH—LOCATIONS IN 29 STATES
bajafresh.com

- Burrito Mexicano (ditch the meat and cheese)
- Burrito Ultimo (hold the meat, cheese, and sour cream)
- Diablo Burrito (skip the meat and cheese)
- Grilled Veggie Burrito (nix the cheese)
- Grilled Veggie Fajitas (ditch the sour cream)
- Pronto Guacamole

- Salsa
- Side salad (skip the cheese)

BASKIN-ROBBINS—NATIONAL CHAIN
baskinrobbins.com

- Daiquiri Ice (and other ices as available; note: BR sherbets contain milk)

BEN & JERRY'S—LOCATIONS IN 38 STATES, PLUS DISTRICT OF COLUMBIA
benjerry.com

- Sorbets
- Smoothies made with sorbets

BENNIGAN'S—LOCATIONS IN 12 STATES
bennigans.com

- Apple pecan salad (ditch the cheese)
- Boca burger
- Garden salad (skip the cheese)
- Roasted vegetable primavera (nix the lemon-butter sauce)
- Spinach salad (nix the bacon, cheese, and egg)
- Steamed broccoli
- Sweet potato fries (only if desperate)

BLIMPIE—LOCATIONS IN 47 STATES
blimpie.com

- Breads—ciabatta, honey oat bread, marble rye bread, whole-grain-wheat bread, spinach tortilla
- Customize a sub with choice of banana peppers, olives, lettuce, tomato, onion, roasted red peppers,

hot peppers, jalapeño peppers, and other veggies; plus guacamole (in moderation)
- Garden salad (no cheese)
- Veggie Salad Sub (no cheese, light or no oil)
- Veggie Supreme Sub (hold the cheese, light or no oil)

BOB EVANS—LOCATIONS IN 23 STATES
bobevans.com

- Apple cranberry spinach salad (lose the chicken) with reduced-fat raspberry vinaigrette
- Applesauce
- Baked potato (skip the butter and sour cream)
- Farmhouse garden salad (minus the cheese) with low-fat balsamic vinaigrette
- Fresh fruit salad plate (nix the yogurt)
- Steamed broccoli

BOSTON MARKET—LOCATIONS IN 30 STATES
bostonmarket.com

- Cinnamon apples
- Cranberry walnut relish
- Fresh steamed vegetables
- Fruit salad
- Garlic dill new potatoes (request without Butter Blend)
- Green beans (request without Butter Blend)
- Mediterranean salad (skip the chicken and feta cheese)
- Rice pilaf
- Southwest Santa Fe salad (nix the chicken and cheese) with sweet garlic vinaigrette

- Sweet corn (request without Butter Blend)
- Tossed salad (nix the croutons)
- Zucchini marinara

BRAVO CUCINA ITALIANA—LOCATIONS IN 20 STATES
bravoitalian.com

- Bravo chopped salad (skip the cheese)
- Grilled vegetable pasta (skip the parmesan)
- Insalata Mista (nix the cheese)
- Insalata Rustica (omit the pancetta)
- Pasta pomodoro with chicken (nix the chicken)
- Vegetable pizzas and flatbreads (minus the cheese)

NOTE: The whole-grain pasta contains eggs; the regular pasta is vegan.

BRUEGGER'S BAGEL BAKERY—LOCATIONS IN 26 STATES
brueggers.com

- Black bean soup
- Build-your-own veggie salad
- Build-your-own veggie sandwich
- Chile cilantro soup
- Fresh-cut fruit salad
- Garden split-pea soup
- Garden Veggie bagel sandwich
- Gazpacho
- Honey grain bagel
- Hummus

- Leonardo da Veggie sandwich (nix the cheese and cream cheese)
- Mandarin salad (ditch the bleu cheese crumbles)
- Marcello minestrone soup
- Mustard
- Pumpernickel bagel
- Ratatouille soup
- Toppings: lettuce, tomato, onion, sprouts, green pepper, and cucumber
- Whole-wheat bagel

BURGER KING—NATIONAL CHAIN
bk.com

- Side garden salad with light Italian dressing
- French fries (only if desperate)

NOTE: The BK Veggie burger contains dairy products.

CAFÉ RIO MEXICAN GRILL—LOCATIONS IN ARIZONA, CALIFORNIA, COLORADO, IDAHO, MARYLAND, MONTANA, NEVADA, UTAH, VIRGINIA, AND WYOMING
caferio.com

- Bean and rice burrito (ditch the cheese)
- Café Rio salad (ditch the cheese) with cilantro-lime vinaigrette
- Guacamole
- Salsa

CALIFORNIA PIZZA KITCHEN—LOCATIONS IN 30 STATES
cpk.com

- Any thin-crust vegetable pizza without the cheese; choose from the following sauces: pizza marinara, vegetarian black beans, or spicy marinara
  - Request whole-wheat crust, where available
- Asparagus arugula salad (nix the cheese)
- Caramelized peach salad (nix the cheese)
- Dakota Smashed Pea and Barley Soup
- Field greens salad
- Lettuce wraps (request only with Chinese vegetables)
- Quinoa and arugula salad with fat-free balsamic vinaigrette (nix the cheese)
- Roasted vegetable salad
- Salad dressings: fat-free balsamic, lemon herb vinaigrette, and sweet & sour
- Tomato basil spaghettini
- Tuscan hummus
- Vegetarian pizza without cheese (thin crust only; request whole-wheat crust, if available)
- White corn guacamole and chips

CALIFORNIA TORTILLA—LOCATIONS IN DELAWARE, MARYLAND, PENNSYLVANIA, VIRGINIA, AND DISTRICT OF COLUMBIA
californiatortilla.com

- No-Meato Burrito
- Sautéed Veggie Fajita (hold the sour cream)

- Southwestern salad with black beans (hold the cheese and sour cream) with light olive oil vinaigrette
- Veggie & Beans Taco (hold the cheese)

CARRABBA'S—LOCATIONS IN 30 STATES
carrabbas.com

- Bruschette (nix the cheese)
- Insalata Fiorucci (hold the cheese)
- Pasta Sostanza (replace with tagliarini; nix the breadcrumbs)
- Penne Franco (replace with tagliarini; hold the cheese)
- Spaghetti Pomodoro (replace with tagliarini)
- Tag Pic Pac (tagliarini with Picchi Pacchiu sauce)

NOTE: Tagliarini is the only dry pasta (therefore made without eggs); substitute all pastas for tagliarini.

CARL'S JR.—LOCATIONS IN 16 STATES, MOSTLY IN THE WEST AND SOUTHWEST
carlsjr.com

- Garden side salad (ditch the cheese and croutons) with low-fat balsamic dressing
- Onion rings (only if desperate)
- Sweet-potato, Natural-Cut, and CrissCut fries (only if desperate)
- Veg It–Fried Zucchini (only if desperate)
- Veg It–Guacamole Burger (skip the cheese, meat, and bacon; request extra veggies and guacamole)

**CHEEBURGER CHEEBURGER—LOCATIONS IN
20 STATES**
cheeburger.com

- French fries (only if desperate)
- Onion rings (only if desperate)
- Grilled portabella mushroom salad with fat-free raspberry vinaigrette
- Grilled portabella mushroom sandwich (hold the cheese)
- Salad Lover's Salad (hold the cheese and creamy dressings)
- Veggie burger
- Veggie burger salad (no cheese) with fat-free raspberry vinaigrette

**CHEESECAKE FACTORY—LOCATIONS IN
34 STATES AND DISTRICT OF COLUMBIA**
thecheesecakefactory.com

- Arugula salad (skip the cheese)
- Beet salad (ax the cheese)
- Broccoli (ask for steamed)
- Edamame
- Endive salad (ditch the cheese)
- Factory chopped salad (nix the chicken and cheese)
- French country salad (nix the cheese)
- Fresh vegetable salad (hold the cheese)
- Greek salad (hold the cheese)
- Little house salad
- Mushroom lettuce wraps
- Pasta marinara

- Santorini Farro Salad (hold the feta cheese and tzatziki)
- Sautéed snow peas and vegetables
- SkinnyLicious Fresh Vegetable Salad (omit the cheese)
- SkinnyLicious Pear & Endive Salad (ditch the cheese and chicken)
- SkinnyLicious Veggie Burger (omit the mayo)
- Steamed asparagus
- Tossed green salad
- White bean hummus, served with warm flatbread
- Wild mushroom flatbread

CHICK-FIL-A—NATIONAL CHAIN
chick-fil-a.com

- Chargrilled chicken and fruit salad (nix the chicken and cheese) with fat-free honey-mustard dressing
- Chargrilled chicken garden salad (nix the chicken, cheese, and croutons) with reduced-fat berry balsamic vinaigrette
- Fruit cup
- Multigrain oatmeal
- Side salad (nix the cheese) with fat-free honey-mustard dressing
- Southwest chargrilled salad (nix the chicken and cheese) with light Italian dressing
- Waffle potato fries (only if desperate)

CHILI'S—NATIONAL CHAIN
chilis.com

- Black beans
- Caribbean or Santa Fe salad without chicken,

shrimp, or cheese, and with fat-free honey-mustard dressing
- Corn on the cob (request without butter)
- Corn tortillas
- Fresh veggies (request without butter)
- Guacamole
- House salad (no cheese or croutons) with fat-free honey-mustard dressing
- Pico de gallo
- Rice
- Steamed broccoli (request without butter)
- Tostada chips (in moderation) and salsa
- Vegetable fajitas
- Veggie quesadillas (minus the cheese and sour cream)

CHIPOTLE—LOCATIONS IN 43 STATES, PLUS DISTRICT OF COLUMBIA
chipotle.com

- All tomato salsas
- Burrito Bowl without beef, chicken, cheese, or sour cream (order extra black beans)
- Corn salsa
- Guacamole
- Salad (minus the meat, cheese, and sour cream)
- Soft tacos with black beans and veggies (hold the cheese and sour cream)
- Veggie burrito (hold the cheese and sour cream)

NOTE: Avoid the pinto beans, which are cooked in bacon, and the non-vegan chipotle-honey vinaigrette.

COLD STONE CREAMERY—NATIONAL CHAIN

coldstonecreamery.com

- Lemon, tangerine, raspberry, and watermelon sorbet.

DAIRY QUEEN—NATIONAL CHAIN

dairyqueen.com

- Applesauce
- Banana
- Chillers and Arctic Rush slushies
- Side salad

DENNY'S—NATIONAL CHAIN

dennys.com

- Applesauce
- Baked potato
- Broccoli, Fiesta Corn, green beans, red-skinned potatoes, sautéed spinach (request without butter)
- Cranberry apple chicken salad (nix the chicken)
- Fit Fare Veggie Skillet (nix the eggs)
- Fresh fruit
- Garden salad (hold the cheese and croutons)
- Grits
- Oatmeal
- Onion rings (if desperate)
- Seasoned fries and french fries (only if desperate)
- Tomato slices
- Veggie burger
- Veggie Skillet (nix the eggs)

DOMINO'S PIZZA—NATIONAL CHAIN
dominos.com

Crunchy thin, whole-grain crust with pizza sauce and any/all fresh veggies

DUNKIN DONUTS—NATIONAL CHAIN
dunkindonuts.com

- Hash browns (only if desperate)
- Multigrain bagel
- Peanut butter (where available)
- Wheat bagel

EINSTEIN BAGELS—LOCATIONS IN 34 STATES
einsteinbros.com

- Fresh veggies
- Fruit cup
- Good grains bagel
- Honey whole-wheat bagel
- Honey whole-wheat bagel thin
- Hummus
- Jelly
- Peanut butter
- Potato bagel

EL POLLO LOCO—LOCATIONS IN 18 STATES
elpolloloco.com

- BRC (beans, rice, cheese) Burrito (ditch the cheese)
- Corn on the cob

- Cucumber salad
- Flour spinach- and tomato-flavored tortillas
- Guacamole
- Pinto beans
- Salsa
- Side salad (hold the cheese)
- Spiced apples
- Ultimate Bowl (nix the chicken, cheese, and sour cream)

EXTREME PITA—LOCATIONS IN 19 STATES, PLUS DISTRICT OF COLUMBIA
extremepita.com

- Falafel (go lightly, as these are typically fried)
- Greek salad (hold the cheese) with balsamic vinaigrette
- Veggie Pita

FRIENDLY'S—LOCATIONS IN 16 STATES
friendlys.com

- Apple Harvest Chicken Salad (ditch the chicken and cheese) with light balsamic vinaigrette
- Garden salad (no cheese or croutons) with fat-free Italian vinaigrette

NOTE: The Boca burger contains dairy.

HÄAGEN-DAZS—LOCATIONS IN 30 STATES AND DISTRICT OF COLUMBIA

haagen-dazs.com

- Sorbets
- Sorbet sippers

GOLDEN CORRAL—LOCATIONS IN 42 STATES

goldencorral.com

This chain's ample buffet features many vegan choices, including:

- Apple cobbler
- Asian green beans
- Baby corn
- Baked potato
- Baked sweet potato
- Breaded okra
- Candied orange slices
- Green beans
- Pagoda stir-fry vegetables
- Penne pasta
- Red beans and rice
- Refried beans
- Rice
- Spaghetti
- Steamed broccoli
- Steamed cauliflower
- Sugar snap peas
- Turnip greens
- Yellow squash
- Zucchini

HARD ROCK CAFÉ—LOCATIONS IN 25 STATES AND DISTRICT OF COLUMBIA
hardrock.com

- Seasonal veggies
- Side house salad
- Veggie Leggie burger (grilled portabella mush-rooms, zucchini, yellow squash, and roasted red pepper; toss the mayo)

JASON'S DELI—LOCATIONS IN 28 STATES
jasonsdeli.com

- Build a sandwich with hummus and veggies on 9-grain artisan bread
- Cajun Nut Mix Cup
- Cranberry Walnut Mix Cup
- Fresh fruit cup
- Garden sandwich (no cheese)
- Guacamole
- Mediterranean wrap (ditch the turkey)
- Nutty Mixed-Up Salad (hold the cheese)
- Organic vegetarian vegetable soup
- Salad bar
- Salsa
- Steamed veggies

JOHNNY ROCKETS—LOCATIONS IN 30 STATES, PLUS DISTRICT OF COLUMBIA
johnnyrockets.com

- French fries (only if desperate)
- Garden salad (skip the cheese)
- Grilled mushrooms

- Onion rings (only if desperate)
- The Streamliner (vegan Boca Burger)

KENTUCKY FRIED CHICKEN—NATIONAL CHAIN
kfc.com

- Corn on the cob (no butter)
- Green beans (no butter)
- House salad with Hidden Valley Garden Italian light dressing
- Potato wedges (make these a rare treat, as they are full of fat, calories, and sodium)

KW CAFETERIAS—LOCATIONS IN NORTH CAROLINA, SOUTH CAROLINA, VIRGINIA, AND WEST VIRGINIA
kwcafeterias.com

- Green salad topped with raw vegetables
- Pasta (whole grain preferred), potato, or brown rice with grilled or steamed vegetables
- Vegetable medley

LE PEEP—LOCATIONS IN 14 STATES
lepeep.com

- Asian salad (nix the chicken)
- Baby Breakfast Burrito (veggies only) with guacamole and salsa
- Breakfast Banana Split (skip the yogurt)
- Cilantro Lime salad (no chicken)
- Dutch Apple Oatmeal
- Garden salad (skip the croutons)

- Granola cranberry oatmeal
- Le Fresh Fruit Ball (skip the yogurt)
- Smoothies: Strawberry Fields, Chuck Berry, Caribbean Cruise
- Strawberry Patch Salad (skip the cheese and chicken)
- Zeus Salad (skip the cheese and chicken)

LONGHORN STEAKHOUSE—LOCATIONS IN 33 STATES
longhornsteakhouse.com

- Baked potato (ditch the butter and sour cream)
- Fresh seasonal vegetables
- Fresh steamed asparagus and green beans (no butter)
- Mixed green salad (nix the cheese and croutons) with balsamic vinaigrette
- Strawberry and pecan salad (no cheese)
- Sweet potato (nix the butter and sour cream)

MANHATTAN BAGEL—LOCATIONS IN 17 STATES
manhattanbagel.com

- Bagels: multigrain, honey whole wheat, power, and pumpernickel
- Fresh fruit salad cup
- Garden Market Salad with Asian dressing
- Village Veggie Sandwich (ditch the cream cheese and chipotle mayo)

MAOZ—LOCATIONS IN TEXAS, FLORIDA, NEW JERSEY, NEW YORK, AND PENNSYLVANIA
maozusa.com

- Belgian fries (only if desperate)
- Falafel on whole-wheat pita with hummus, eggplant, and tahini (in moderation, as falafel is typically fried)
- Fill with your choice of condiments, including baba ganoush, chickpea salad, broccoli-and-cauliflower medley, olives, and beets
- Tabouli salad

MAUI TACOS—LOCATIONS IN CALIFORNIA, HAWAII, IDAHO, MARYLAND, MINNESOTA, NEVADA, NEW JERSEY, NEW YORK, NORTH CAROLINA, TEXAS, AND DISTRICT OF COLUMBIA
mauitacos.com

- Haiku Burrito (hold the cheese and sour cream)
- Maui Vegetarian Taco (hold the cheese and sour cream)
- Paia Surf Burrito
- Puamana Surf Burrito (hold the cheese)
- Vegetarian Bowl

MCALISTER'S DELI—LOCATIONS IN 22 STATES IN SOUTH, SOUTHWEST, AND MIDWEST
mcalistersdeli.com

- Green salad with fresh vegetables, dried cranberries, and honey-roasted almonds, topped with fat-free chipotle peach dressing

- Spicy guacamole
- Vegetarian chili with harvest wheat bread
- Vegetarian club (hold the parmesan peppercorn sauce)
- Veggie spud (hold the cheese)

MCDONALD'S—NATIONAL CHAIN
mcdonalds.com

- Apple slices
- Fruit and walnut salad (ditch the yogurt)
- McVeggie Burger (available only in New York City, California, and Canada)
- Side salad with low-fat balsamic dressing

MOE'S SOUTHWEST GRILL—LOCATIONS IN 35 STATES
moes.com

- Art Vandalay vegetarian burrito (ditch the cheese and sour cream)
- Homewrecker or Joey Bag of Donuts burrito with tofu (skip the cheese and sour cream)
- Overachiever, Funk Meister, or Unanimous Decision taco (ditch the cheese and sour cream)
- Personal Trainer Salad (nix the cheese)
- The Fat Sam Fajita with tofu
- Tofu Rice Bowl (minus the cheese)
- Customize your meal with these options:
  - All tomato salsas
  - Black beans
  - Guacamole
  - Jalapeños
  - Lettuce (salad)

- Olives
- Pinto beans
- Soft corn tortilla
- Tofu
- Vegetables

NOODLES & COMPANY—LOCATIONS IN 18 STATES, PLUS DISTRICT OF COLUMBIA
noodles.com

- Chinese Chop Salad (hold the wontons)
- Indonesian Peanut Sauté
- Japanese Pan Noodles
- Penne Rosa (hold the cream and the cheese)
- Spaghetti (hold the cheese)
- Whole-Grain Tuscan Linguine (hold the cream and the cheese)

OLIVE GARDEN—NATIONAL CHAIN
olivegarden.com

- Capellini* with pomodoro or tomato sauce
- Garden Fresh salad with oil and vinegar (skip the cheese and croutons)
- Minestrone soup
- Steamed veggies (request without seasoned butter)

Other pastas on the menu contain egg.

OUTBACK—NATIONAL CHAIN
outback.com

- Baked potato (nix the butter and sour cream)
- Baked sweet potato (nix the butter and sour cream)

- Fresh steamed broccoli, green beans, and mixed veggies (order without butter)
- Grilled asparagus (request without butter)
- House salad (omit the cheese and croutons) with fat-free tangy tomato dressing

PANERA BREAD—LOCATIONS IN 40 STATES
panerabread.com

- Apple
- Classic salad (without cheese)
- Fandango salad (without cheese)
- Greek salad (no cheese), reduced-fat balsamic vinaigrette dressing
- Low-fat black-bean soup
- Low-fat garden vegetable soup (without pesto) with slice of whole-grain artisan bread
- Mediterranean veggie sandwich (without cheese) on whole-grain artisan bread
- Portabella and mozzarella sandwich (without cheese) on whole-grain artisan bread
- Strawberry poppy-seed salad (without chicken)
- Whole-grain bagel

PAPA JOHN'S—NATIONAL CHAIN
papajohns.com

- Vegetarian pizza (minus the cheese)

PEI WEI ASIAN DINER—LOCATIONS IN
9 STATES
peiwei.com

- Caramel with vegetables, tofu, and brown rice
- Edamame
- Honey Seared with vegetables, tofu, and brown rice
- Japanese teriyaki noodle/rice bowl
- Sesame with vegetables, tofu, and brown rice
- Side of vegetables
- Spicy Korean with vegetables, tofu, and brown rice
- Sweet and Sour with vegetables, tofu, and brown rice
- Thai Coconut Curry with vegetables, tofu, and brown rice
- Thai Dynamite with vegetables, tofu, and brown rice
- Vegetable and tofu pad Thai (request without egg)
- Vegetable spring rolls

NOTE: The menu uses a leaf symbol to denote dishes made without meat or animal products. Request Stock Velvet (steamed) preparation.

P.F. CHANG'S—LOCATIONS IN 25 STATES
pfchangs.com

- Asian tomato-cucumber salad
- Brown rice
- Buddha's Feast with vegetables and tofu (order steamed)
- Coconut Curry Vegetables
- Edamame
- Edamame dumplings

- Garlic snap peas
- Lemon-scented Brussels sprouts
- Ma Po Tofu
- Shanghai cucumbers
- Spinach stir-fried with garlic
- Spring rolls
- Steamed vegetable dumplings
- Stir-fried eggplant
- Vegetable Chow Fun
- Vegetarian fried rice (request no egg)
- Vegetarian lettuce wraps

PIZZA HUT—NATIONAL CHAIN
pizzahut.com

- Veggie Lover's pizza with multigrain crust (omit the cheese)

QDOBA—LOCATIONS IN 40 STATES
qdoba.com

- All tomato salsas
- Black beans
- Brown rice (in select locations)
- Grilled veggies
- Guacamole
- Lettuce (salad)
- Pinto beans
- Soft corn tortilla
- Taco with grilled vegetables
- Tortilla soup
- Whole-wheat tortillas

QUIZNOS—NATIONAL CHAIN

quiznos.com

- Fresh Garden Salad Bowl with fat-free balsamic vinaigrette
- Create your own veggie sub on artisan wheat bread—choose from tomatoes, red onions, black olives, mushrooms, cucumbers, green bell peppers, banana peppers, jalapeños, pickles, lettuce, guacamole; top with fat-free balsamic vinaigrette

RED LOBSTER—LOCATIONS IN 46 STATES

redlobster.com

- Asparagus (request no butter)
- Baked potato (hold the butter and sour cream)
- Garden salad with balsamic vinaigrette
- Linguine with marinara sauce
- Pico de gallo
- Red wine vinaigrette
- Steamed broccoli
- Wild rice pilaf

ROMANO'S MACARONI GRILL—LOCATIONS IN 41 STATES

macaronigrill.com

- Cappellini pomodoro
- Garden Della Casa salad (nix the cheese) with balsamic vinaigrette dressing
- Grilled asparagus and broccoli
- Mediterranean olives
- Penne arrabiata (no cheese)

- Spinach and garlic
- Tomato bruschetta (nix the cheese)
- White peach sorbet

NOTE: Macaroni Grill's fresh and whole-wheat pastas are not vegan; stick with cappellini.

ROY ROGERS—LOCATIONS IN MARYLAND, MASSACHUSETTS, NEW JERSEY, NEW YORK, PENNSYLVANIA, AND VIRGINIA
royrogersrestaurants.com

- Baked apples
- Baked potato (ditch the butter and sour cream)
- Fruit salad
- Garden salad (hold the cheese)
- Mashed potatoes (nix the gravy and butter)
- Salad bar—choose veggies and low- or fat-free dressing

RUBY TUESDAY—LOCATIONS IN 47 STATES
rubytuesday.com

- Create Your Own Garden Bar (tons of vegan options)
- Grilled zucchini, grilled green beans, grilled asparagus, steamed broccoli, baked potato, sugar snap peas, roasted spaghetti squash (make sure all are prepared without butter)
- Spaghetti squash marinara (hold the parmesan)
- Veggie Trio

SANDELLA'S FLATBREAD CAFÉ—LOCATIONS IN 25 STATES, PLUS DISTRICT OF COLUMBIA

sandellas.com

- Apple walnut salad (hold the cheese) with light balsamic vinaigrette
- Artichoke grilled flatbread (hold the cheese)
- Black Beans & Rice Bowl (hold the cheese)
- Cucumber and tomato wrap
- Greek salad (hold the feta) with light balsamic vinaigrette
- Hummus wrap
- Napa Valley salad (hold the cheese) with light balsamic vinaigrette
- Paradise Crunch salad
- Santa Fe salad (hold the cheese) with light balsamic vinaigrette
- Siesta salad with light balsamic vinaigrette
- Tomato and cucumber salad (hold the cheese) with light balsamic vinaigrette
- Vegetable Confetti grilled flatbread (hold the cheese)
- Veggie Ranch wrap (swap ranch dressing for light balsamic vinaigrette)

SHEETZ—LOCATIONS IN MARYLAND, NORTH CAROLINA, OHIO, PENNSYLVANIA, VIRGINIA, AND WEST VIRGINIA

sheetz.com

- French fries (only if desperate)
- Garden salad (no cheese) with fat-free Italian dressing

- Taco salad (nix the chili and sour cream) with fat-free Italian dressing and/or condiments (salsa, pico de gallo, guacamole)

STARBUCKS—NATIONAL CHAIN
starbucks.com

- Multigrain bagel
- Perfect Oatmeal
- Roasted vegetable panini (hold the cheese)
- Sesame noodles (comes with broccoli, carrots, peanuts, pickled cucumbers, red pepper, snap peas, and tofu)
- Starbucks also sells vegan chocolates, granola bars, and nuts

SUBWAY—NATIONAL CHAIN
subway.com

- Nine-grain wheat bread with
  - Any fresh veggies
  - Guacamole (in moderation)
  - Fat-free sweet onion dressing
  - Mustard

TACO BELL—NATIONAL CHAIN
tacobell.com

- 7-Layer burrito (nix the cheese and sour cream)
- Bean burrito (hold the cheese)
- Fiesta taco salad (nix the meat, cheese, and sour cream)
- Guacamole
- Mexican pizza (nix the cheese, meat, and sour cream)

- Salsa
- Soft tacos (hold the meat, cheese, and sour cream; add beans)
- Tortilla chips
- Veggie fajita wrap (ditch the cheese)

TACO DEL MAR—LOCATIONS IN 24 STATES
tacodelmar.com

- Black bean and corn salsa
- Guacamole
- Mondito Burrito (ditch the cheese and sour cream) with salsa
- Pico de gallo
- Rice and black beans

TEXAS ROADHOUSE—LOCATIONS IN 40 STATES
texasroadhouse.com

- Baked potato (no butter or sour cream)
- Baked sweet potato (no butter or sour cream)
- Country Veg Plate (make sure it's prepared without butter)
- House salad (no cheese and egg)
- Seasoned rice

T.G.I. FRIDAY'S—NATIONAL CHAIN
tgifridays.com

- Broccoli
- Classic Mediterranean hummus with warm pita bread
- Pecan-crusted chicken salad (ditch the chicken and cheese)

- Strawberry Fields salad (ditch the cheese) with low-fat balsamic vinaigrette
- Sweet potato fries (only if desperate)
- Vegetable medley

TIM HORTON'S—LOCATIONS IN INDIANA, KENTUCKY, MAINE, MARYLAND, MICHIGAN, NEW YORK, OHIO, PENNSYLVANIA, VIRGINIA, AND WEST VIRGINIA
timhortons.com

- 12-grain bagel
- Hearty vegetable soup
- Mixed berry smoothie without yogurt
- Oatmeal with mixed berries
- Wheat and honey bagel

WENDY'S—NATIONAL CHAIN
wendys.com

- Apple pecan chicken salad (nix the chicken and cheese)
- Baja salad (nix the chicken, tortilla chips, chili, and tortilla chips) with fat-free French dressing
- Baked potato with extra broccoli; no cheese, butter, or sour cream
- Berry almond chicken salad (nix the chicken and cheese)
- French fries (only if desperate)
- Garden side salad (no cheese or croutons) with fat-free French dressing
- Mandarin oranges

- Veggie sandwich—basically a burger without the burger, but includes all the trimmings (lettuce, tomato, onion, pickle, and so forth)

***WHOLE FOODS*—LOCATIONS IN 38 STATES**

wholefoodsmarket.com

EAT-IN OPTIONS INCLUDE:

- Salad bar
  - Beans
  - Fruit
  - Grains (like brown rice and quinoa)
  - Greens
  - Seeds
  - Veggies
  - Vinegar, soy, or oil-free dressing
- Fresh soups
  - Adobe black vegan
  - Vegetarian chili
  - Check other veggie-based soups for ingredients

ACKNOWLEDGMENTS

We would jointly like to thank author, actor, and dear McComsey family friend Jim McMullan for believing in our idea so much, he introduced us to our future agent, Janet Rosen of Sheree Bykofsky Associates. Jim and his wife, Helene, have been great supporters throughout the process. We are grateful to Janet for her wit, creativity, and interest in veganism—and for her many great suggestions that made our proposed book more tantalizing. We are also indebted to Lisa's lifelong friend and attorney extraordinaire, Raymond Moss, who guided us through foreign territory—the contract legalese— while he was juggling a million other things. Enormous thanks to Amy's friend, mentor, and client, Dr. Caldwell Esselstyn, who supported our project from its inception and graciously agreed to write our foreword. We send a heartwarming shout-out to our excellent "amateur" editors, including Stanley Amelkin, Alicia McComsey, Meg Rosen, Shannon Stovsky, Christopher Torpey, and Alexandra Wagner, who offered candid feedback, creative ideas, and loads of encouragement. Finally, we thank our talented and enthusiastic editor at Penguin Group, Jeanette Shaw, who helped us pull it all together. It has been a joy to work with her.

Amy Cramer

First and foremost, I thank Dr. Caldwell Esselstyn and his fabulous wife, Ann. Without them, this book would not exist. They have forever changed my life—as well as the lives of countless others—with their tireless work in spreading the dire health concerns of our planet and the absolute need for a plant-based lifestyle. Their constant encouragement and support led me to first become a vegan, then a professional vegan chef, and now an author.

I thank my mom for always encouraging (and pushing) me to cook and write. I fell in love with the magic of the kitchen due to your welcoming support. Thanks to my dad for also being a damn great cook, as well a loyal believer that I could do anything, And of course, thank you to my sister, Liz, who places me on a pedestal and laughs at all of my jokes; you are my sunshine!

A warm thank you to my wonderful husband, Ken, for always loving my cooking, even when it looked like brown mush, and for always believing that I could succeed at whatever I tried. Thank you also to my three fabulous kids for not screaming too loudly when I gently encouraged them (ha!) to test my newest creations. The three of you are the greatest gift a mom could ever want.

A huge thank you to my dear family and friends old and new, who have always loved and supported me. An extra thank-you to my tireless sous-chef testers, Meg Rosen and Miriam McCarty. A special thanks to Jamie Cole for pushing me to pursue my dreams and to Peter Jacobson for his endless kitchen expertise.

Last, but definitely not least, an enormous thank you to my fabulous coauthor, Lisa. From our early days of running together in Central Park then eating meatballs and sausage to our current days of vegan creating, cooking, and writing, I have loved every minute of the journey. I can't wait to see where it takes us next.

Lisa McComsey

Thank you to my amazing family—parents, Ed and Alicia, and siblings, Scott, Leslie, and Marisa and their respective significant others and kids—who have stood by me throughout my vegan journey, never once rolling their eyes or dissing my decision. In spite of their ongoing love for bacon and cheese, they've shown unwavering support and continually demonstrate openness and curiosity—always eager to try plant-based recipes and patronize vegan restaurants. You are my rock. And Mom, thanks for being my tireless PR agent!

My wonderful friends and colleagues have been equally loving and gracious, and I am grateful to each and every one of you. Special thanks to my running buddy, John Mecchia, who, over our many miles together on the Seaside boardwalk, has given me untold hours of wisdom, entertainment, and inspiration. After listening to my vegan ramblings, he, too, "switched teams" and is now a plant-eating running machine.

I would not have embarked on this journey without my coauthor and longtime friend, Amy, whose own vegan story inspired me to give it a shot. Soon after my conversion, she asked me to collaborate on a how-to-govegan book. It has been a joy to partner with my former *People* magazine colleague, with whom I'd spent several years running, eating, and dishing when we both lived in New York. She is energetic, motivating, and a blast to work with. You have changed my life. Thank you!

RESOURCES

BOOKS

General Vegan

Becoming Vegan, by Brenda Davis, RD, and Vesanto Melina, MS, RD (Book Publishing Company, 2000)

The China Study, by T. Colin Campbell, PhD, and Thomas M. Campbell II (Ben Bella Books, 2004)

The Engine 2 Diet, by Rip Esselstyn (Wellness Central, 2009)

Food for Life, by Neal Barnard, MD (Three Rivers Press, 1993)

Living Vegan for Dummies, by Alexandra Jamieson, CHHC, AADP (Wiley Publishing, 2010)

Prevent and Reverse Heart Disease, by Caldwell B. Esselstyn Jr., MD (Penguin Group, 2007)

Skinny Bitch, by Rory Friedman and Kim Barnouin (Running Press Book Publishers, 2005)

Thrive: The Vegan Nutrition Guide to Optimal Performance in Sports and Life, by Brendan Brazier (Da Capo Press, 2009)

Veganist: Lose Weight, Get Healthy, Change the World, by Kathy Freston (Weinstein Books, 2011)

The Vegan Sourcebook, by Joanne Stepaniak, MS Ed (Lowell House, 1998)

Cookbooks

Candle 79 Cookbook: Modern Vegan Classics from New York's Premier Sustainable Restaurant, by Joy Pierson, Angel Ramos, and Jorge Pineda (Ten Speed Press, 2011)

Let Them Eat Vegan!: 200 Deliciously Satisfying Plant-Powered Recipes for the Whole Family, by Dreena Burton (Da Capo Press, 2012)

The 30-Minute Vegan, by Mark Reinfeld and Jennifer Murray (Da Capo Press, 2009)

The Sexy Vegan Cookbook, by Brian L. Patton (New World Library, 2012)

Vegan Cooking for Dummies, Alexandra Jamieson, CHHC, AADP (Wiley Publishing, 2011)

Vegan Cupcakes Take Over the World, by Isa Chandra Moskowitz, Terry Hope Romero, and Sara Quin (Da Capo Press, 2006)

Veganomicon, by Isa Chandra Moskowitz and Terry Hope Romero (Da Capo Press, 2007)

Vegan Planet, by Robin Robertson (Harvard Common Press, 2003)

WEBSITES

American Vegan Society—americanvegan.org

Dreena's Vegan Recipes—viveleveganrecipes.blogspot.com

Fat-Free Vegan Kitchen—fatfreevegan.com

Finding Vegan—findingvegan.com

Happy Cow—happycow.net

Kris Carr: Home of the Crazy, Sexy Wellness Revolution—kriscarr.com

Manifest Vegan—manifestvegan.com

Vegan and Gluten-Free—xgfx.org

The Vegan Cheat Sheet—vegancheatsheet.com

Vegan Eating Out—veganeatingout.com

VeganHealth.org

Vegansaurus!—vegansaurus.com

VegDining.com

Vegetarian Resource Group—vrg.org

VegGuide.org

Veg Kitchen with Nava Atlas—vegkitchen.com

VegSource.com—vegsource.com

VegVine—vegvine.com

MAGAZINE

VegNews—published six times a year by VegNews Media
(vegnews.com)

INDEX

ABOUT THE AUTHORS

Susan Woog Wagner Photography

AMY CRAMER, Vegan Chef, Coach, Instructor, and Entrepreneur

Following a five-year stint as a marketing executive at *People* magazine, Amy founded a fitness-based direct-marketing company, Highpoint Communications, which she eventually sold. After she and her husband, Ken, converted to veganism in 2007 to combat Ken's chronically high cholesterol, Amy launched the Cleveland-based vegan chef service Dinners Done Now. As owner and head chef, she prepared weekly vegan meals for three-hundred-plus clients, among them the Esselstyn family (Rip Esselstyn is author of the vegan bestseller *The Engine 2 Diet*; his father, Caldwell B. Esselstyn

Jr., MD, penned *Prevent and Reverse Heart Disease*). After moving to Boulder, Colorado, in July 2011, she founded Vegan Eats, which produces a line of grab-and-go vegan meals for supermarket chains and online ordering (veganeatsusa .com). Amy has taught private vegan classes throughout Ohio, and in New York City and Westchester County, New York, and has been a guest lecturer at Bronx Community College. She also offers one-on-one vegan coaching to those who need more guidance and handholding. Whole Foods Market frequently invites her as a guest instructor. A rising vegan culinary celebrity, Amy is frequently cited in food and health blogs and has been touted in the local press. She lives with her husband and three children—Cai, Liv, and Cam—in Boulder, Colorado.

Susan Woog Wagner Photography

LISA McCOMSEY, Writer, Marketing Consultant, and Public Speaker

An award-winning copywriter, Lisa has worked on staff and as a freelance copywriter for a variety of publications, including *Vogue, People, Life, Real Simple, Vanity Fair, Bon Appétit, GQ, House & Garden, Brides, House & Garden,* the *New York Times,* and *Every Day with Rachael Ray,* and currently serves as copy director for *Allure* magazine. She co-owned a marketing company for seven years before venturing off on her own as a freelance writer and marketing consultant in early 2010 (see LisaMcComsey.com). A two-time recipient of the Time Inc. President's award, Lisa is also an award-winning Toastmaster speaker. She cultivated a love for rice and beans while living in Costa Rica and Baja, Mexico, during a three-year volunteer teaching stint—giving her a taste of what was to come when she decided to go vegan in 2009. An avid bicyclist and runner, Lisa has completed twenty-four marathons, several century rides, and a handful of triathlons. After growing up at the Jersey Shore and vowing "never to go back" once graduated from high school, Lisa returned to her roots and happily resides a few miles from the ocean.